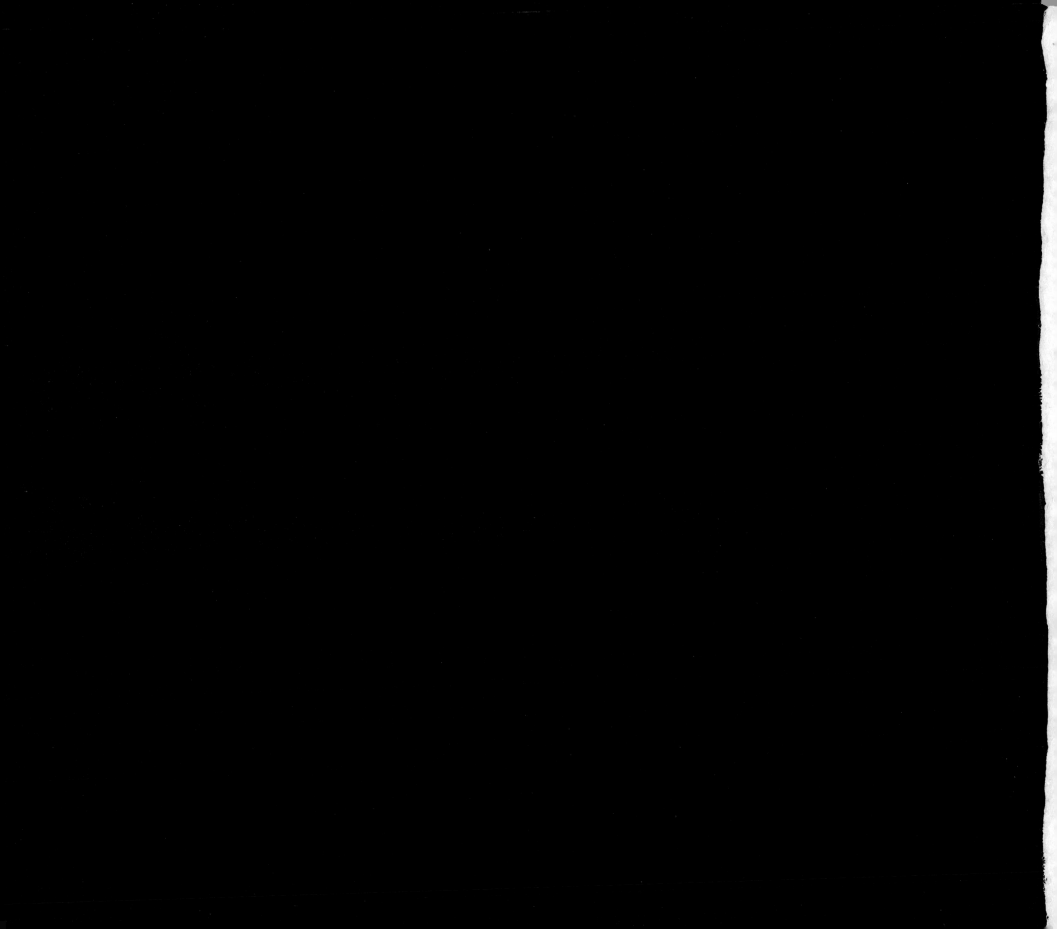

A&D WEJCHERT & PARTNERS

A&D WEJCHERT & PARTNERS

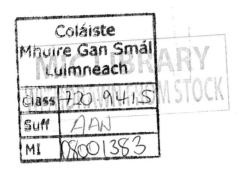
ISBN 978 0948037 559

Essays by Tadeusz Barucki, Cathal O'Neill, Raymund Ryan
French translations by Marie Ange Zakrzewska
Archive photos reproduced by Repro 35
Digital illustrations processed by Gunther Berkus
Printed by Nicholson & Bass, Belfast

cover – Helix Performing Arts Centre, Dublin City University
(photo: Peter Moloney)
frontispiece – Sobanski Palace Complex, Warsaw
(photo: Wojciech Krynski)

Published and distributed by Gandon Books
Oysterhaven, Kinsale, Co Cork, Ireland
T +353 (0)21-4770830 / F +353 (0)21-4770755
E gandon@eircom.net / W www.gandon-editions.com

A&D WEJCHERT & PARTNERS, ARCHITECTS
23 Lower Baggot Street, Dublin 2, Ireland
T +353 (0)1-6610321 / F +353 (0)1-6610203
E mail@wejchert.ie / W www.wejchert.ie

Contents

l'Architecture est le grand livre de l'humanité

—Victor Hugo

Foreword

WE CONSIDER OURSELVES VERY FORTUNATE TO HAVE HAD THE OPPORTUNITY to design a great variety of structures with functions as diverse as education, tourism, healthcare and worship. The resulting cross-fertilisation of ideas from one type of project to another enriches the designs and adds elements of surprise.

Of course, designing for different purposes demands an understanding of the parameters governing the human activities and functions that will occur within those structures. Therefore our ethos involves continual research into the ever-changing and developing needs of the human beings who will use those structures, together with the discovery of new technological solutions. That combination is what makes our practice of architecture such a fascinating endeavour.

As we respond to the needs of society and reflect that spirit in formal expression, we consciously strive to make a significant contribution to the latest chapter in that great book of humanity called architecture.

opposite – Quinn Direct, Blanchardstown, Dublin

Avant-Propos

NOUS NOUS ESTIMONS EXTREMEMENT PRIVILEGIES D'AVOIR EU LA POSSIBILITE de travailler sur un grand nombre de projets variés répondant a des besoins très divers tels que l'éducation, le tourisme, la santé ou le culte religieux. L'interaction des idées qui en découlent et qui se mélangent d'un projet à l'autre enrichit la création et provoque des éléments de surprise.

Bien sûr, la création s'adressant à des activités si diverses entraîne la connaissance de ces paramètres gouvernant les activités humaines et les fonctions prenant place au cœur même de ces structures. Notre philosophie est donc de rester en permanence à l'écoute de l'évolution et du développement des besoins des utilisateurs de ces structures, en parallèle avec celles des nouvelles technologies. Cette dualité est ce qui rend notre métier en architecture aussi fascinant.

En répondant aux besoins de la société et en donnant forme à ces principes, nous nous efforçons lucidement de participer au dernier chapitre de ce grand livre de l'humanité qu'est l'architecture.

Introduction

PROFESSOR CATHAL O'NEILL

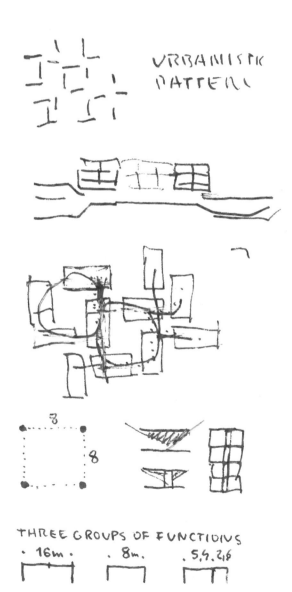

ANDRZEJ WEJCHERT GRADUATED IN WARSAW IN 1962 AND BEGAN WORKING IN A SPECIAL DIVISION WITHIN THE STATE office responsible for school design. In his spare time he also began entering international competitions, including that for a new campus for University College Dublin at Belfield. In 1964 he planned to travel to France to see the great works of the masters and to visit his fellow architect, Danuta Kornaus, who had gone to Paris to study at the Ecole des Beaux-Arts. The week before Andrzej was due to leave for Paris, he received a telegram from Ireland informing him that he had won first prize in the competition for the Belfield campus. He was invited to Dublin to collect his prize and to immediately begin arrangements for building the project. He simply did not believe the telegram until he received a second, more urgent message convincing him that it was not a mistake. And so he took the Paris train but disembarked in Amsterdam instead. There, he went straight to the airport with all his belongings packed into two suitcases and bought a one-way ticket to Dublin. On checking in, his luggage was found to be over the weight limit and, having no money, was faced with the choice of leaving one of the cases behind. The first contained all his clothes and the second all his precious books. Inevitably, he arrived in Ireland with a case full of books and nothing more than the suit he was travelling in.

When he landed in Ireland, the college authorities were astonished to discover that it was such a young architect with only a few years experience who had won this prestigious competition. Andrzej explained that he would be delighted to carry out the work in hand provided he could go into association with an Irish firm. He interviewed the various firms on offer and chose Robinson Keefe Devane – a very wise choice. Andy Devane, the partner who was assigned to the project, and his associate Roddy McCaffrey were experienced and talented architects. Andy had studied with Frank Lloyd Wright, and Roddy had worked for Harrison & Abramovitz on the UN building in New York.

Andrzej's success against 126 competitors from 46 countries – including many established firms – was a remarkable achievement, especially given the difficult conditions in architectural education and architectural practice at that time in Poland. Fortunately, some excellent teachers in the school had experienced the Modern movement before the war, and indeed it was one of those teachers who subsequently helped place Andrzej in the state's department for school design when he graduated. There, perhaps because of his energy and talent, he was given his first chance to design a large school. Not built at the time, it was built and published some years later, so it is not surprising then that in addition to his success in the university competition, he should have many education buildings in his port-

opposite – Irish Cement offices, Drogheda

Original (1963) sketches for University College Dublin competition folio. Danuta Kornaus's early career followed a similar path. On graduation, her first job was as an architect with the state's department responsible for the design of health facilities.

Belfield is probably the Wejchert's most important project: it brought Andrzej to Ireland, it developed his professional skills, and won him the Triennial Gold Medal of the Royal Institute of the Architects of Ireland (the premier award of the profession). It firmly established his practice and led to new commissions on the Belfield campus and elsewhere. But it was also a project of some controversy, architecturally and otherwise. There existed considerable opposition to the moving of UCD from its original city-centre location to one in the suburbs.

The site for the competition had a very strong field pattern, which the architect proposed would be reinforced with dense planting to create a series of 'gardens', each of which would have a faculty building. The importance of the landscaped enclosures was emphasised in Wejchert's submission and was essential to the success of the plan. Unfortunately the subsequent planting, although extensive, did not adhere to this concept, and the departure from the master plan in the placement of some buildings has led to an open and somewhat fragmented composition of the elements, lacking the landscape framework which would have given cohesion to the place and provide comforting shelter from the wind.

Many years later, in 1986, the Wejcherts created a miniature sample of what might have been in Belfield when they designed the landscape for the courts at Fitzwilliam Lawn Tennis Club. Here a strict grid (dictated by the court dimensions) of 3m-high clipped yew hedges encloses each of the courts, forming sheltered outdoor rooms of simple beauty and practical effectiveness.

During the ten years or so of the construction of the Belfield competition buildings, the Wejcherts made a number of important decisions that established their future together in Ireland. Firstly, Danuta agreed to move to Ireland despite the fact that her real goal was to work in the USA. Significantly, Danuta insisted from the start on working independently from Andrzej, and took a job in Robinson Keefe Devane, where she learned quickly about Irish construction methods. Over time, they both gained sufficient confidence to open their own practice, A&D Wejchert Architects, in 1974.

Despite a heavy workload, they made time to enter numerous competitions and had a high rate of success, winning awards in the Department of Education school competition and the Dublin Diocesan church competition, both of which led to further commissions. The practice has continued to enter competitions throughout the world, and although their ideas have often been rewarded with prizes, one suspects that their primary motive was not so much to win or to generate new work, but rather to explore new ideas and practice virtuosity in the manner of the musical études of their compatriot Chopin.

A study of their competition entries is rewarding, for it reveals a different order of response to the problems posed than that of their built work. Here the work is freer, open-ended, filled with a sculptural expression employing a surprising range of materials. It is as though they see competitions as an opportunity to enjoy a freedom of expression, unhindered by the constraints of today's architectural practice. For example, in their competition entry design for the 20th-Century Museum in Japan, the major events of the last century are laid out along the course of a symbolic river of life, passing through a large rectangular space above which are suspended transparent glass tubes containing the 'products of the mind'. The glass floor of the upper space makes possible a visual link to past times, while the glass ceiling above provides views of the heavens. With this simple device, the complex relationships between thought, action and time are fused with a simple and elegant construction.

In the competition for an aquarium in Nouméa, Nouvelle Calédonie (for which they were shortlisted), the Wejcherts draw on a crustaceous form to produce a striking building, the walls and roof of which are curved sections of pale-grey metal panels interspaced with translucent glass strips, with a glazed rooflight over the centre of the building. A complex section provides the necessary daylight for the exhibits and shaded areas for the visitors. The whole building appears alive, like a giant crab moving slowly down the beach to the sea. And yet there is no sense of deception, of architecture copying nature, but rather a beautiful man-made construction inspired by creatures of the sea.

Proposed aquarium in
Nouméa, Nouvelle Calédonie

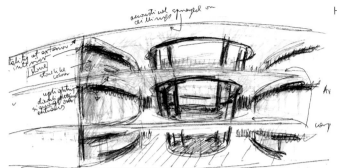

An example of their built work can be seen at The Helix, the arts centre at Dublin City University – a delightful addition to the new campus. The three performing spaces are grouped, like leaves of a shamrock, around a foyer on three levels, dominated by a circular colonnade containing the grand circular stairs. The whole space, which is filled with light and movement, can be enjoyed as theatre by the public. The theatrical entertainments are placed against a backdrop, as it were, of a long, narrow building containing the offices, studios and services, which, in turn, is surmounted by and illuminated glazed fly tower. The audiences are well cared for as each of the auditoria has excellent acoustics, sight lines and a sense of warm comfort.

The well-being of patients was the primary motivation in the design of the psychiatric unit at Naas General Hospital, and the deinstitutionalising of the place was part of that programme. Danuta drew on the painted gable-ended houses of the town to create small-scale urban units in contrast to the monolithic workhouses of 1840. Orientation and aspect have been carefully considered to avail of the nearby pond. The overall effect is that of a staggered streetscape in a small town, integrated with the wider community.

The Aillwee Cave Visitor Centre illustrates the architects' preference for a restrained intervention that respects the character of the site – in this case the Burren, and most especially the grandeur of the caves. Regarding this project, Andrzej says, 'we should limit our action on the surface and glorify the earth from within'. Indeed, viewed from the approach road, the building could be mistaken for a natural outcrop on the sheer rock of the hillside; only the gravelled area of the car park and the cars indicate man's presence.

The Administration Building at UCD is an example wherein the physical transparency and democratisation of space has inspired the design. The main hall is the meeting ground where students and the college officers engage to enrol, look for accommodation, receive exam results or seek help. These transactions, which can be complex and stressful, are thoughtfully accommodated in the large square room, two storeys in height, with a ceiling of well-detailed rooflights flooding the space with light, mezzanines on three sides, and views to the campus on the fourth. The open-plan room brings all the staff into full view of the anxious students, and creates a sense of openness to the proceedings.

A broad stairway in the lobby seems to invite students to the upper floors, from where the president directs the business of the college and presides over the academic council, adding to the sense of accessibility. There is a sense in the main hall of Frank Lloyd Wright's Johnson Wax factory, one of the few occasions in Wejchert's work where a direct influence of others may be discerned. Externally, the building adopts the same elevational treatment as the Arts / Commerce Building, which it faces across the mall, with a continuous horizontal window pattern and a projecting spandrel housing the services and which serves as a *brise-soleil*. But here the pattern is interrupted with recesses and tall rectangular columns to express the hall and accommodate the change in ground level.

The Wejcherts are also capable of witty architectural statements. The small offices for the Irish Cement company near Drogheda, set in the midst of the silos of the plant, is a delightful example of *trompe d'oeil*. The architects' Corbusier-like sketches illustrate their attempts to obscure, or at least diminish the scale of the tall cylindrical silos. The use of curved, free-standing, concrete walls, solid and perforated, succeeds in this while giving a masterclass in concrete construction.

In the mid-1990s, the Wejcherts returned to Poland to undertake their first commission there, the Media Business Centre, an office building which, at 32,000m² is the same size as the Arts / Commerce and Administration buildings at UCD, built thirty

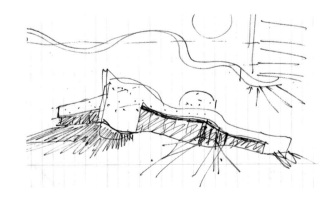

Media Business Centre
for ITI, Warszawa
– sketch of the final version

years earlier. Like the Belfield building, it has been suitably praised and honoured. In 1999 they completed the restoration of the Sobanski Palace and the bold insertion of a new office building into the courtyard. This may be the best work that the practice has done to date. The new building, with its delicate façade of vertical and horizontal louvres, is the ultimate in glass architecture. It stands in the deep snow like a giant block of ice that had been chiselled and polished to a glistening form of virtual perfection. It won them an award from the Polish Minister of Culture, the title of Best Public Building in Warsaw, 1998-99, and encouraged architects to aim higher.

They have an opportunity to do so in their latest Polish project – a mixed-use development, a vast shopping centre dominated by a diaphanous tower. The concept for the shopping centre is also unusual. Instead of the fortress-like form of most centres, where the shopping is introverted towards ubiquitous malls, here the ground-floor shops face outwards and are surmounted by large polygonal panels which seem suspended in space like a line of flags in a Kurosawa film. The tall tower and the mass of the shopping centre will form a striking composition, a modern version of hill town and tower.

The success of the Wejcherts' work is unsurprising given their talent, hard work and good fortune. Since their first commission in 1964 they have designed 90 projects, almost all built to a consistently high standard, even when money was scarce. They have been well served by loyal staff, with six partners – Paddy Fletcher, Martin Carey, Paul Roche, Helen Giblin, David Lanigan and lately Graham Dwyer – some of whom have been with the firm from as early as the 1970s. Their presence has broadened the practice base, allowed it to expand and undertake large work, whilst maintaining attention to clients' needs and quality. Their joint efforts have been applauded by their clients, peers, juries, government bodies, professional institutes, environmental bodies and universities, who have awarded them the highest honours and many repeat commissions.

Their offices are in a 19th-century four-storey Dublin townhouse, to which they have added a modern extension in the garden facing a courtyard shared with the main house. The large high-ceilinged rooms in both buildings house the studios, which have a relaxed yet disciplined atmosphere without the clutter common to architects' workplaces. Andrzej and Danuta each have a tiny office dominated by pin-up wall space displaying sketches and models of their latest projects.

Andrzej is the spokesman for the pair, talking softly with a distinctive Polish accent and a near-perfect command of the English language. Danuta prefers to communicate through her drawings. They both have an attractive old-fashioned politeness, giving you their full attention, and would never dream of taking a phone call in your company. Their philosophy, or work method, as they may prefer to call it, is primarily focused on what generates a building – the client's needs, the site and their own inspiration, drawn, one imagines, from natural forms, geometry and the discipline of materials. They are clearly not fashionistas and they are generous in praise of their fellow Irish architects, especially young architects, without appearing to be influenced by them. They talk about the genius of the great masters, especially Corb and Mies, and occasionally Frank Lloyd Wright, but there is no attempt to emulate them.

The Wejcherts are probably in agreement with the painter Gerhard Richter, who said, 'I want to produce a painting, not an ideology.'

_____

Professor Cathal O'Neill graduated from University College Dublin in 1955, and studied for his Masters degree at the Illinois Institute of Technology under Mies van der Rohe. He later worked for Mies in his private office. He returned to Ireland to practice and teach at UCD, and was head of the School of Architecture from 1973 until 1995. He continues in practice with his son. His book *Cathal O'Neill's Dublin* is a collection of watercolour paintings and commentaries on Dublin's buildings, old and new.

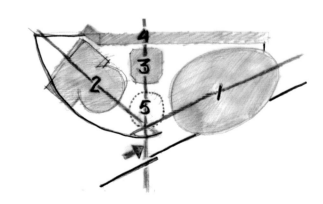

The Helix, DCU – dynamic geometry of (1) concert hall, (2) theatre, (3) experimental theatre and (4) support facilities defines (5) foyer

INTRODUCTION

ANDRZEJ WEJCHERT EST SORTI DIPLOME DE SON ECOLE D'ARCHITECTURE A VARSOVIE en 1962 et a débuté dans sa carrière comme fonctionnaire dans un organisme gouvernemental responsable de la construction d'établissements scolaires. Dans ses temps libres, il a également commencé à participer à des concours internationaux y compris celui d'un nouveau complexe universitaire pour University College à Belfield. En 1964 il projetait de se rendre en France pour voir les chefs-d'œuvre des maîtres et de rendre visite à sa collègue architecte Danuta Kornaus qui était à Paris pour faire ses études à l'Ecole des Beaux-Arts. La semaine précédant son départ, Andrzej a reçu un télégramme d'Irlande lui annonçant qu'il avait gagné le premier prix du concours pour l'université à Belfield. On l'invitait à Dublin pour recevoir son prix et pour commencer la mise en place immédiate du projet. Andrzej n'y a pas cru et il en a fallu un second, beaucoup plus urgent, qui l'a convaincu que ce n'était pas une erreur. Il a alors pris le train pour Paris mais a débarqué à Amsterdam. Il est allé directement à l'aéroport avec toutes ses affaires dans deux valises et a acheté un billet aller simple pour Dublin. A l'enregistrement, ses bagages dépassaient le poids permis et, comme il n'avait pas l'argent nécessaire pour payer le supplément, il a dû choisir et laisser une des deux valises. L'une contenait ses vêtements et l'autre ses précieux livres. Il est donc arrivé à Dublin avec une valise pleine de livres et rien d'autre que le costume qu'il portait.

A son arrivée en Irlande, les autorités du collège ont été stupéfaites de découvrir que c'était un jeune architecte avec seulement quelques années d'expérience qui avait remporté ce concours prestigieux. Andrzej a expliqué qu'il entreprendrait avec plaisir le travail à faire à condition de pouvoir s'associer à un cabinet d'architectes irlandais. Il interviewa différents cabinets candidats et sélectionna Robinson Keefe Devane, un excellent choix. Andy Devane, l'associé désigné pour suivre le projet, et son associé Roddy McCaffrey étaient des architectes de grand talent et expérimentés. Andy avait étudié avec Frank Lloyd Wright et Roddy avait collaboré avec Harrison & Abramowitz sur l'immeuble de l'ONU à New York.

D'avoir remporté le concours sur 126 concurrents de 46 pays, y compris certains cabinets très expérimentés, était remarquable surtout lorsqu'on connait les conditions difficiles de l'enseignement et de l'exercice de la profession en Pologne à cette époque. Heureusement que certains des excellents professeurs de l'école s'étaient initiés au mouvement Moderne avant la guerre, et c'est d'ailleurs l'un d'eux qui a ensuite aidé Andrzej à trouver un emploi dans l'organisme chargé des établissements scolaires. Et c'est là que son énergie et son talent lui ont valu de travailler pour la pre-

mière fois sur un projet important pour une école. Pas encore construite à cette époque, elle l'a été depuis et a fait l'objet de publications quelques années plus tard. Il est donc normal que, en plus de l'université, il ait de nombreux projets de bâtiments scolaires dans ses dossiers. La carrière de Danuta a suivi sensiblement le même trajet. Une fois diplômée, son premier emploi comme architecte a été dans un organisme d'état responsable d'établissements de santé.

Belfield aura sans doute été le projet le plus important pour les Wejchert: il a attiré Andrzej en Irlande, lui a permis de développer ses connaissances et lui a rapporté la Médaille d'or triennal du RIAI (la plus prestigieuse de la profession). Il a également aidé au développement de son cabinet et a conduit à de nouvelles commandes sur le complexe de Belfield et ailleurs. Mais c'était un projet très controversé que ce soit d'un point de vue architectural ou autre. Le déménagement de UCD du centre ville vers un quartier de banlieue soulevait à l'époque, une opposition considérable.

L'endroit sélectionné par le concours avait une très forte identité champêtre que l'architecte désirait renforcer par des plantations denses et créer ainsi une série de « jardins », chacun abritant une faculté. L'importance de ces enclos verts avait été soulignée par les Wejchert dans leur présentation, ces espaces devant assurer le succès du projet. Malgré l'importance de ce qui a été planté, le concept n'a pas été respecté, certains bâtiments n'ont pas été placés comme ils auraient du l'être dans le projet initial et il en résulte aujourd'hui un assemblage d'éléments dispersés auquel manque la structure des plantations qui aurait apporté une certaine cohésion entre les éléments et aurait offert de la protection contre le vent.

Plusieurs années plus tard, en 1986, les Wejchert ont créé un échantillon miniature de ce qui aurait dû être à Belfield en élaborant les plantations pour les cours au Club de Tennis de Fitzwilliam et qui se résume en une grille rigide d'ifs taillés de trois mètres de haut entourant les courts et formant des espaces extérieurs abrités, pratiques et d'une beauté simple.

Pendant les dix ans qu'a duré la construction des éléments du concours à Belfield, les Wejchert ont pris d'importantes décisions qui ont assuré leur avenir commun en Irlande. Tout d'abord, Danuta a décidé de s'installer en Irlande alors que son idée première était de partir travailler aux USA. Très révélateur de son caractère, Danuta avait décidé dès le début de travailler indépendamment d'Andrzej et de prendre un emploi avec Robinson Keefe Devane où elle a rapidement appris les méthodes de construction locales. Ayant tous les deux acquis assez d'assurance au bout de quelques années, ils ont ouvert leur propre cabinet en 1974.

Malgré un programme de travail lourd, ils ont toujours pris le temps de participer à de nombreux concours, dont beaucoup couronnés de succès, et en particulier celui d'un établissement scolaire pour le Ministère de l'Education et celui d'une église pour le Diocèse de Dublin, deux projets qui en ont entraîné d'autres. Le cabinet a continué à répondre aux demandes des concours internationaux et bien que leurs idées aient souvent gagné des prix, leur motivation principale ne semble pas de gagner ou de remporter d'autres commandes mais plutôt d'explorer de nouvelles idées et d'exercer leur talent de virtuoses, comme leur compatriote Chopin dans ses études musicales.

Il est intéressant d'étudier leurs participations aux concours. Elles révèlent des réponses aux problèmes posés, différentes de celles qu'ils apportent dans leur activité de construction. Leur travail est plus libre, plus flexible, sculptural, employant une grande variété de matériaux. C'est comme s'ils voyaient dans les concours la possibilité de s'exprimer librement sans les contraintes de l'exercice de l'architecture moderne. Leur projet pour le Musée du 20ème siècle au Japon illustre bien cette attitude. Les principaux événements du siècle dernier suivent la rivière symbolique de la vie qui traverse un grand espace rectangulaire au-dessus duquel sont suspendus des tubes en verre transparents contenant « les produits de l'esprit ». La base en verre du niveau supérieur permet un lien visuel avec le passé tandis que la partie supérieure, également en verre, offre des perspectives sur les cieux. Grâce à cette formule ingénieuse, les relations complexes entre pensée, action et temps se traduisent facilement en une construction simple et élégante.

Pour le concours d'un aquarium à Nouméa en Nouvelle Calédonie (pour lequel ils ont été présélectionnés) les Wejchert s'inspirent de la forme d'un crustacé pour créer un bâtiment remarquable avec des murs et un toit en sections rondes de panneaux de métal gris clair entrecoupées de bandes de verre translucide, le tout couronné au centre d'une partie vitrée. Un système complexe permet l'éclairage par la lumière du jour de ce qui est à voir et l'ombre pour les visiteurs. Le bâtiment entier semble vivre, se déplaçant lentement le long de la plage vers la mer. On n'éprouve pas l'impression désagréable d'une architecture plagiant la nature mais au contraire celle d'une construction faite par l'homme et inspirée par les créatures de la mer.

Le Helix, le nouveau centre artistique du complexe à Dublin City University, offre un excellent exemple de leurs réalisations. Les trois espaces de performances sont regroupés, telles les feuilles d'un trèfle, autour d'un foyer sur trois niveaux dominé par une colonnade ronde abritant un escalier circulaire. Ce théâtre, espace rempli de lumière et de mouvement, est très apprécié du public. Les performances prennent place avec, comme arrière-plan, un bâtiment long et étroit où sont logés les bureaux, studios et services et d'où s'envole une tour de verre illuminée. Le public jouit d'une excellente acoustique, d'un champ de vision ininterrompu dans chaque auditorium et d'un agréable confort.

Pour l'élaboration du service de psychiatrie de l'hôpital de Naas, le bien-être des patients était au cœur de la réflexion et la déréglementation faisait partie du programme. Danuta s'est inspirée des maisons aux pignons peints de la ville pour créer des unités urbaines à petite échelle à l'opposé des hospices mastoc de 1840. La relation du bâtiment avec un étang proche a influé sur son orientation et son apparence et l'impression générale est celle d'un profil de rue étagé d'une petite ville qui s'intègre facilement dans la communauté.

Le Centre de Visiteurs des grottes de Aillwee illustre bien la prédilection des architectes pour un traitement sobre respectant le caractère du site, et dans ce cas précis: le Burren et la splendeur des grottes. Commentant ce projet, Andrzej dit que « on devrait limiter son intervention à la surface et célébrer la terre de l'intérieur ». En effet vu de la route, le bâtiment ressemble à un affleurement naturel de la roche sur le flanc de la colline, seul le gravier du parking et les voitures signalent la présence de l'homme.

Le bâtiment administratif de UCD illustre très clairement l'influence de la transparence physique et de la démocratisation de l'espace sur l'élaboration d'un projet. La grande salle est le lieu de rencontre des étudiants et du personnel de l'université pour s'inscrire, chercher un logement, vérifier les résultats des examens ou demander de l'aide. Ces rapports qui peuvent être difficiles et angoissants, sont traités dans une grande pièce carrée, haute de deux étages, inondée de lumière venant des nombreuses percées vitrées dans le toit, avec des mezzanines sur trois côtés et la vue sur le campus sur le quatrième. Aucun obstacle ne cache le personnel de la vue des étudiants anxieux ce qui ajoute une grande ouverture aux rencontres. Cette impression d'accessibilité est encore renforcée par un escalier aux proportions généreuses qui semble inviter les étudiants à monter vers les étages supérieurs, là où le Président assure la gestion de l'université et préside au conseil académique. On retrouve, dans cette pièce principale, des affinités avec l'usine de Johnson Wax par Frank Lloyd Wright, l'une des rares occasions où l'on remarque l'influence de certains architectes sur les Wejchert. De l'extérieur, la façade du bâtiment adopte le même style que celui des Arts et Commerce qui lui fait face, avec des bandes ininterrompues de fenêtres à l'horizontale et une projection faisant office de brise-soleil et abritant les services. Mais ici l'uniformité est brisée par des renfoncements et de hautes colonnes carrées qui marquent le pourtour de la salle et intègrent les changements au niveau du sol.

Cependant les Wejchert sont également capables d'humour dans leurs expressions architecturales. Ce petit bureau pour la Irish Cement Company près de Drogheda, planté au milieu des silos de l'usine est un charmant exemple de trompe l'œil. Les sketches des architectes de style Corbusier illustrent parfaitement leurs efforts pour cacher ou au moins diminuer l'échelle de ces grands silos cylindriques. L'utilisation de murs de béton, arrondis, indépendants, en blocs ou percés d'orifices y réussit parfaitement tout en donnant une leçon de maître sur la construction en béton.

Dans les années 1990 les Wejchert sont repartis en Pologne pour mener à bien leur première commande qui s'est trouvée être un bureau de 32,000m², Media Business Centre, la même surface que les bâtiments des Arts et Commerce et Administratif à UCD construits trente ans plus tôt. Comme pour Belfield ce projet a remporté beaucoup de succès.

En 1999, ils ont achevé la restauration du Palais Sobanski et ont mené à bien le projet audacieux d'ajouter dans la cour un nouveau bâtiment. Celui-ci représente sans doute la réalisation la plus admirable réalisée par le cabinet à ce jour. Avec sa façade très délicate de bandes de verre verticales et horizontales, le nouveau bâtiment représente le summum en architecture de verre. Ce bâtiment se dresse dans la neige tel un bloc de glace géant qu'on a sculpté et poli jusqu'à obtenir une forme étincelante proche de la perfection. Le Ministre de la Culture Polonais leur a décerné un prix, le bâtiment a été nommé le meilleur bâtiment Public à Varsovie en 1998-99 et a encouragé les architectes à être plus exigeants.

Leur projet polonais le plus récent va leur donner la possibilité de se surpasser. Il s'agit d'un développement à usage multiple, un grand centre commercial dominé par une tour diaphane. Le concept pour la partie commerciale est également original. Au lieu d'un centre à l'aspect de forteresse où la partie commerciale tourne sur elle-même le long de grandes avenues, dans ce projet les boutiques du rez-de-chaussée sont tournées vers l'extérieur, surmontées par de grands panneaux aux multiples côtés suspendus en l'air comme une ligne de drapeaux dans un film de Kurosawa. La tour qui s'élève au-dessus de la masse du centre va composer un ensemble remarquable, comme une version moderne d'un village montagneux et de sa tour.

Le succès des Wejchert ne surprend pas. Ils le doivent à leur talent, leur travail acharné et leur chance. Depuis leur première commande en 1964, ils ont conçu 90 projets, presque tous construits, et toujours d'un très haut niveau, même quand les budgets étaient limités. Ils ont été très aidés par un personnel fidèle et six associés – Paddy Fletcher, Martin Carey, Paul Roche, Helen Giblin, David Lanigan et dernière-

ment Graham Dwyer. Certains travaillent dans le cabinet depuis les années 70. Leur participation a permis de donner plus d'envergure au cabinet. Elle lui a permis de se développer et d'entreprendre de grands projets tout en restant à l'écoute des besoins des clients et en maintenant un travail de qualité. Leurs efforts ont été loués par leurs clients, par leurs pairs, par les jurys, les organismes gouvernementaux, les instituts professionnels, les associations de l'environnement et les universités qui leur ont décerné les plus grands honneurs et leur ont passé des commandes à plusieurs reprises.

Ils ont leurs bureaux dans une maison de ville de Dublin du dix-neuvième siècle, de quatre étages à laquelle ils ont ajouté une annexe dans le jardin autour d'une cour intérieure. Les studios se trouvent dans des pièces aux hauts plafonds où règne une atmosphère calme mais disciplinée, sans le désordre habituel des bureaux d'architectes. Andrzej et Danuta y ont chacun un tout petit bureau aux murs couverts de sketches et maquettes de leurs derniers projets.

Andrzej est le porte-parole des deux, parlant doucement avec une trace d'accent polonais et un anglais pour ainsi dire parfait. Danuta préfère communiquer par le biais de ses dessins. Ils sont tous les deux d'une politesse d'antan, très séduisante. Ils se consacrent entièrement à vous et n'envisageraient jamais de répondre à un appel téléphonique en votre présence. Leur philosophie, ou comme ils préfèrent la nommer, leur méthode de travail, se concentre sur ce qui fait un bâtiment, les besoins du client, le terrain et leur propre inspiration qui vient, comme on peut l'imaginer, des formes trouvées dans la nature, de la géométrie et de la discipline des matériaux. Ils ne sont certainement pas intéressés par les modes et se montrent généreux dans leurs éloges envers leurs collègues irlandais, surtout les jeunes mais sans être particulièrement influencés par eux. Ils parlent du génie des grands maîtres, surtout Corb et Mies, et à l'occasion Frank Lloyd Wright, mais ne tentent pas de les imiter.

Les Wejchert seront sans doute d'accord avec le peintre Gerhard Richter qui dit: « je veux produire un tableau et non une idéologie ».

———

Professeur Cathal O'Neill a fait ses études d'architecture à University College Dublin où il a passé son diplôme en 1955. Il a continué avec la préparation d'une Maîtrise en Architecture sous la direction de Mies van der Rohe à l'Institute of Technology d'Illinois. Il a ensuite travaillé pour Mies van der Rohe dans son agence. Revenu en Irlande, il a ouvert son propre cabinet d'architecture et a dirigé l'Ecole d'Architecture de UCD de 1973 à 1995. A ce jour, il poursuit ses activités avec son fils qui l'a rejoint dans son cabinet. Son livre *Cathal O'Neill's Dublin* est une collection d'aquarelles et de commentaires sur les bâtiments de Dublin, anciens et modernes.

UCD campus at Belfield, 1973

Community School, Ballincollig, Co Cork

Andrzej Wejchert and Danuta Kornaus-Wejchert
(photographed in 1980 by Tadeusz Barucki)

Danuta and Andrzej Wejchert

TADEUSZ BARUCKI

IT ALL STARTED IN 1964 WITH THE SUCCESS IN AN INTERNATIONAL ARCHITECTURAL COMPETITION AT UNIVERSITY COLLEGE Dublin. The first prize went to a young up-and-coming Polish architect, Andrzej Wejchert. Undertaking the difficult task of bringing the prize-winning design to fruition in totally new surroundings, not quite aware of the local conditions and professional regulations, he met with obstacles that could be overcome thanks only to the exceedingly friendly co-operation of his Irish colleagues, something that Wejchert has retained in his grateful memory until today. The first stage in building the Arts/Commerce Building proved the value of the design manifested in the competition. The next stage in the extension of the university – the Administration Building (completed in 1972) – was recognised as the best building in recent years and awarded the RIAI Gold Medal, presented to the Polish architect by the President of Ireland. This reaffirmed Wejchert's position and prompted him to settle on Irish soil. While working on the expansion of the University, the Wejcherts (since 1966 Andrzej Wejchert has worked in collaboration with his wife and former fellow student at the Technical University in Warsaw, Danuta Kornaus) have taken part in numerous architectural competitions. Their work, taken together, reveals the evolution of an interesting idea, a kind of foundation for Andrzej and Danuta's production to rest on. It can be traced back to a school in Plock, built to Wejchert's design.

The idea concerns an organisation of space that takes into account the relation between a small group of people or an individual and a larger community. 'An individual', says Wejchert, 'is too often lonely and lost in a crowd.' This aspect is seen most clearly in the couple's designs for school buildings, and it is no accident that these are the subjects that are most frequently dealt with on the Wejchert's drawing boards. Beginning with the school in Plock, through the design for University College Dublin, for Calabria University (prepared for a competition), the extension of University College Cork (Ireland) – now being designed – to the newly built schools in Ballincollig and Ballynanty in Ireland, this compositional idea can be seen through all the Wejcherts' works.

These two schools reveal two further interesting aspects of their innovatory approach to function, material and construction. The popular principle of the elastic transformation of school interiors according to current needs has been additionally enriched by a movable cabin, a teacher's room, which, placed in an appropriate position, can impose a natural and desired division upon a classroom. As regards construction, the architects used plastics as their building material. Elements of the walls, ceiling and roofs are mass-produced in this very material, satisfying the requirements of both thermal insulation and construction resistance. The material also provides an important colour tone. The rich colour scheme offered by modern chemistry has been consciously limited by the architects to a single tone. In the first of the schools, the colour chosen is yellow with shades of brown, which, says Danuta Wejchert, is intended as a link between the architecture of the school and the characteristic colour of the broom shrubs growing around the building. The other school is dominated by shades of red, which corresponds with the roof tiles of the neighbouring housing estate. This is the first time this technology has been used in Ireland, and Danuta and Andrzej Wejchert are using it again in their design for a centre for various small industries.

To depart a little from the mainstream of the Wejcherts' interests, let us mention other designs: the entrance to the Aillwee Cave, integrated in its outer aspect with the unique surroundings. Next, the design for Herbert von Karajan's house on water (prepared for a competition), and, first and foremost, the fascinating, reinforced concrete water tower in the grounds of University College Dublin, and Holy Trinity Church, Dublin. In the latter, the elements are made of cast glass, and owing to their matte rough texture, give rise to striking visual effects. The triangular forms prevailing in the construction have prompted architecture British critics to seek a literary association with the name of the church. I think that the two latter designs reveal the individual creative attitudes of each of the architects. The sculpture of the water-tower reflects Andrzej's style, and Danuta's church, lyrical in its purely tectonic quality, reflects her formal creativeness.

It is pleasant to recommend the output of people whose letterhead, apart from the abbreviations standing for the Irish and British institutes of architects, bears also that of the Union of Polish Architects. It was also greatly satisfying to see the astonishment of the jury awarding the prize of the International Architects Union (I was one of the judges) having learnt that the Irish candidate to the Perret Prize was the Polish architect Andrzej Wejchert. And though the prize was awarded *ex aequo* to the French team Rogers & Piano, and the Japanese architect Kikutake, the fact that Ireland suggested a Polish architect working in that country is very telling.

Tadeusz Barucki is an architect and architectural critic, and a recipient of the l'Union International des Architects Jean Tschumi Prize for his contribution to international architectural education.

This essay was first published in *Projekt* (Warszawa), °136, March 1980, pp.30-35

Aillwee Cave Visitor Centre, Co Clare

O'Rahilly Building, UCC

Water Tower, UCD

Holy Trinity Church, Dublin

ANDRZEJ ET DANUTA WEJCHERT

Tout a commencé en 1964, par un succès au concours international d'architecture à University College Dublin. Andrzej Wejchert, jeune architecte polonais, au seuil de sa carrière (né en 1937, études à l'Université technique de Varsovie), a obtenu le premier prix. Il ne pourrait mener à bien la tâche difficile de l'exécution du projet lauréat dans un milieu inconnu, sans l'aide amicale de ses confrères irlandais. La première étape de la réalisation, appelée Arts/Commerce Building, a confirmé les qualités du projet. La deuxième étape – l'agrandissement de l'Université avec le bâtiment des bureaux – réalisée en 1972, a été reconnue comme la meilleure réalisation des dernières années et récompensée d'une médaille d'or remise par le président d'Irlande. Ceci a évidemment encouragé l'architecte polonais à s'installer en Irlande. Parallèlement à l'agrandissement de l'Université, le couple d'architectes (car Andrzej Wejchert trave depuis 1966 avec sa femme, Danuta Kornaus née en 1938, une camarade d'études), prend part à de nombreux concours d'architecture. Leurs projets rassemblés documentent l'évolution d'une idée intéressante qui constitue une sorte de fondement de l'oeuvre architecturale d'Andrzej et de Danuta Wejchert. Des embryons de cette idée sont visibles dans l'école réalisée par Wejchert à Plock, en Pologne.

Cette idée consiste en un aménagement de l'espace qui prend en considération le rapport entre un petit groupe, un individu même, et une collectivité. « L'individu » dit Wejchert « est trop souvent seul et perdu dans la foule ». Le problème est d'autant plus visible à l'école et ce n'est pas par hasard qu'il est devenu le thème principal présent sur les planches à dessin des Wejchert. En commençant par l'école le Plock, le projet de University College Dublin, le projet envoyé au concours de l'Université de Calabre, le sérieux agrandissement de University College Cork en Irlande, jusqu'aux écoles réalisées à Ballincolling et Ballynanty en Irlande – les travaux des Wejchert sont nettement inspirés par l'idée d'une telle composition.

Les deux dernières écoles révèlent en outre des aspects intéressants d'une solution novatrice des fonctions, des matériaux et de la construction. Le principe connu de la transformation élastique des intérieurs scolaires pour répondre à des besoins immédiats, a été enrichi par l'élément mobile d'une cabine-pièce pour le maître, qui, convenablement manoeuvrée, peut d'une manière naturelle faire place à une classe. Des matières plastiques servent de matériau de construction. Les éléments des murs, des planchers et des toits sont faits industriellement de ce matériau qui répond aux exigences de l'isolation thermique et de la résistance. La couleur du matériau joue également un grand rôle. La même technologie, qui fut appliquée pour la première fois en Irlande, sert à Dublin à la construction d'une halle projetée par Andrzej et Danuta Wejchert, qui abritera des établissements de petite industrie.

Citons encore d'autres projets qui s'écartent quelque peu de ce que font les Wejchert, par exemple rentrée de la Grotte Aillwee, dont la forme extérieure cadre parfaitement avec le paysage unique qui l'entoure, ensuite le projet présenté au concours de la villa sur l'eau de Herbert von Karajan, et surtout l'étonnant château d'eau en béton armé sur le territoire de University College Dublin, ainsi que l'église Sainte Trinité de Dublin.

C'est un plaisir que de parler de l'acquis de créateurs dont l'en-tête du papier à lettres porte les sigles des Instituts irlandais et britannique des Architectes, ainsi que celui de la Société des Architectes polonais. Et quelle satisfaction que l'étonnement du dernier jury du Prix Perret attribué par l'Union internationale des Architectes, auquel je participais, quand les jurés se sont rendu compte que le candidat irlandais est l'architecte polonais Andrzej Wejchert. Et bien que cette fois le prix soit allé ex aequo au groupe français de Roger Piano et au Japonais Kikutake, la présentation par l'Irlande de la candidature d'un Polonais se passe de commentaires.

Tadeusz Barucki est architecte et critique et a reçu le prix Jean Tschumi décerné par l'Union Internationale des Architectes pour la critique et l'enseignement de l'architecture au niveau international.

L'essai a été publié dans la revue *Projekt*, °136, 3/80 (Varsovie, 1980)

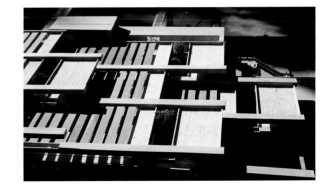

Universita degli Studi della Calabria, Italy – competition

Eclectic Geometries: A&D Wejchert in Ireland and Poland

RAYMUND RYAN

MATHEMATICS IS CENTRAL TO THE PRACTICE OF ANDRZEJ AND DANUTA WEJCHERT, WHETHER ADDITION — THE ASSEMBLY of elements – or subtraction – the erosion of pure volumetric form. Their work uses geometry pragmatically, to assist processes of construction, and symbolically, as a signal in its own right of loftier architectural ambition. If this co-existence of the rational and abstract Rationalism has a continental flavour, it may in part result from affinities between Polish and French cultures. Warsaw, for instance, is a city that has, at various stages, wanted to be more like Paris. Indeed, in its heyday inter-war period, Polish architecture evoked a belief and pleasure in geometry ranging from folkloric pattern (art nouveau or National Romanticism) to Constructivist planning.

Since moving to Ireland from Poland in 1964, after Andrzej won the master-plan competition for University College Dublin at Belfield, the Wejcherts have contributed impressively to Irish architecture. Over a span of now four decades, their projects reveal an intellectual curiosity about contemporary architectural theories and languages. They exhibit eclectic affinities that include Brutalism and the megastructural (as with Belfield); experimental prefabricated components (Ballincollig school; AnCo, Loughlinstown); Rural Organicism (Aillwee Cave); Postmodern composition (office blocks on Abbey and Lower Mount streets in Dublin); and now neo-Modern plastic form, as with the recently completed Media Business Centre in suburban Warsaw and The Helix Performing Arts Centre at Dublin City University.

Back in 1964, the emigrés found a professional home at Robinson Keefe Devane. Today they describe Andy Devane and Roddy McCaffrey as 'our teachers ... their attitude was so tolerant.' Whilst it is tempting to connect a symbiosis in their work of the geometric and the organic to some Wrightian spirit at work in Robinson Keefe Devane during the 1960s, that practice also gave the young Poles a base or structure from which to analyse local professional reality. After all, it seems characteristic of the Wejchert practice – established in 1974 after such key constituents of Belfield as the Arts Block, bank and Administration Building were complete – to not only test out new styles or ideas, but to implement these proposals. The only other immigrant architect with comparable levels of expectation – the Australian Raymond McGrath – met with considerably less success.

With their team of now five partners, Andrzej and Danuta Wejchert continue to brave the often fickle world of competitions, both in Ireland and abroad. Most recently they proposed for the Waterford quays a pattern of splayed vectors to separate built and open zones, 'treating the river as a big living room' with a vitreous cultural facility beck-

Sobanski Palace Complex, Warszawa

oning 'like a TV'. No other Irish practice has participated in quite so many foreign competitions, from that for the Vienna International Organisations and Conference Centre in 1969 (totemic monoliths containing stacked terrace floors) to a new university in Calabria, Italy. For that university they imagined a Cartesian superstructure of classrooms above a shaded, undulating terrain settled by communal spaces – an exemplary coexistence of the rationalist and natural.

Successive entries to Japan's Shinkenchiku ideas competition included first a tripartite tower with three circular pods suspended above the Mediterranean (envisaged for maestro Herbert von Karajan). Then a museum of the 20th century, where transverse transparent boxes – each containing key artefacts for one decade – hovered above a more fluid timescape on which one might track major historical themes as if pathways in a garden. In the Baggot Street office today are many competition drawings and models, retained as talismans, perhaps, or triggers for conceptual development in subsequent designs. In an inverse way, the Aillwee Cave Visitor Centre influenced their Hong Kong Peak proposal in 1983 with a semi-interred, hollow ziggurat camouflaged against the hillside by striated bands of planters.

In the 1990s the Wejcherts returned to build in Poland. The Sobanski Palace is situated on Aleje Ujazdowskie, one segment of a boulevard that links the Royal Palace in Warsaw's Old Town to the Enlightenment Summer Palace at Wilanow some ten kilometres south. It's a prestigious thoroughfare with affinities to both Edinburgh's Royal Mile and the great Cartesian axis that aligns the Louvre through what is now La Defense to Louis XIV's estates west of Paris. The Palace has its own Gallic flavour, symmetrically composed with twin gatehouse pavilions and formal garden elements. Now a private club, the building has been elegantly renovated. The Wejcherts excavated the basement and surrounding adjacent areas so that natural light illuminates the lowest levels with kitchens and services accommodated underground outside the palace footprint.

North Quay Venue Building,
Waterford – competition

To one side of the Palace, against the wall of the British Embassy, the practice then constructed a prismatic three-storey pavilion perpendicular to the boulevard that is skinned in glass and screened from low sun by external glass louvres. Another Polish project is the Media Business Centre, south from the Sobanski Palace towards Wilanow. Combining TV studios, video distribution facilities and Internet company offices within a stepped cubic form, the Centre's façades are glazed similarly to those of the Sobanski Palace pavilion. The Centre however is far bigger. It contains two light-filled atria, one raised an entire storey above the other and both roofed in a vast curving glass canopy. Geometry is here at the service of sociability, the atria sided in large, sliding windows so that views and light spread throughout the organism.

There may in such iterations by the Wejchert practice be some affinity with the accumulative tactics of Dutch architect Herman Hertzberger. The modular glass-reinforced polyester schools at Ballincollig and Ballynanty, fabricated in the 1970s by a boat builder on the Isle of Wight and arriving 'like a travelling circus', are arranged in circular or orphic fragments whereby the encircled and interstitial spaces are harnessed for communal purpose. Such Dutch Structuralists as Hertzberger and, earlier, Aldo van Eyck structured architectural plans as 'organigrams', dispositions of cognitive form between which fields of shared activity (playtime for children, informal meetings for adults) could occur The Media Business Centre is in this sense a crystal hive waiting to be animated by multiple patterns of daily use.

The Helix at DCU is not dissimilarly a battery of three sealed and distinct performance spaces, plus a background bar of more normative supplementary rooms. Its figure/ground condition offers alternate readings of the curvaceous interstitial foyer, as void – as residual space between the three concave chambers – and solid – as a vertical promenade and pivot for the entire complex. With a rooftop, blue-lit cube off rather jauntily to one side, The Helix is also some kind of multi-dimensional billboard, displaying itself to the campus and passers-by on Collins Avenue. With its curved surfaces suggesting movement and hospitable form, The Helix is again an exercise in clear geometric composition, a further manifestation of the Modernist desire for light and form achieved amid the cut-and-thrust of contemporary Irish reality.

Raymund Ryan is curator at the Heinz Architecture Center, Pittsburgh, Pennsylvania. He is author of *Cool Construction* (Thames & Hudson, London, 2001) and co-author of *Building Tate Modern* (Tate Publishing, London, 2000), and has written extensively on Irish and international architecture.

This essay was first published in *Architecture Ireland*, °183, January 2003, pp.34-35

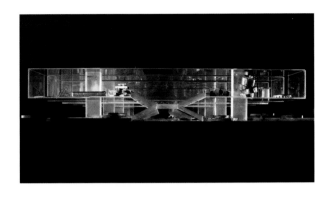

20th-Century Museum, Japan

Community School,
Ballincollig

Media Business Centre for ITI,
Warszawa

The Helix, DCU
– detail of foyer

Raymund Ryan, conservateur
du Heinz Architecture Centre
de Pittsburgh en Pennsylvanie,
est l'auteur de *Cool
Construction* (Thames &
Hudson, Londres, 2001). Il a
également contribué à
Building Tate Modern (Tate,
Londres, 2000) et à de
nombreux écrits sur
l'architecture en Irlande et à
l'international.

L'essai a été publié dans
Architecture Ireland, °183,
janvier 2003.

DE L'ECLECTISME ET DE LA GEOMETRIE:
A&D WEJCHERT EN IRLANDE ET EN POLOGNE

LES MATHEMATIQUES SONT AU CŒUR DES ACTIVITES DU CABINET D'ARCHITECTURE DE Andrzej et Danuta Wejchert, que ce soit des additions – l'ajout d'éléments – ou des soustractions – l'érosion des volumes purs. Dans l'exercice de leur activité, ils utilisent la géométrie d'une façon pragmatique pour aider les procédés de construction et d'une façon symbolique comme signe d'une haute ambition architecturale. Si cette coexistence du rationnel et du Rationalisme abstrait a un caractère européen, cela tient sans doute en partie aux affinités entre les cultures françaises et polonaises. Varsovie, par exemple est une ville qui avait comme ambition à différentes époques de mieux ressembler à Paris. En effet, dans sa période faste d'entre les deux guerres, l'architecture polonaise exprimait sa confiance en la géométrie et son plaisir à l'utiliser allant des modèles inspirés du folklore (Art Nouveau ou Romantisme National) ou du Constructivisme.

Andrzej ayant remporté le concours du grand projet de University College Dublin à Belfield en 1964, les Wejchert sont arrivés en Irlande et ont contribué au développement de l'architecture irlandaise d'une façon remarquable. Depuis maintenant plus de 40 ans, leurs projets font preuve d'une curiosité intellectuelle concentrée sur les théories et l'interprétation de l'architecture contemporaine. Ils font preuve de liens éclectiques allant du Brutalisme et des grandes structures (Belfield par exemple), aux prototypes de composants préfabriqués (l'établissement scolaire de Ballincollig et bâtiment AnCo à Loughlinstown), à l'Organisme rural (la Grotte Aillwee), et à la composition Postmoderne (immeubles sur Abbey Street et Mount Street) pour en arriver actuellement à la forme plastique Néomoderne du Centre de communication à Varsovie et de celui de l'Helix à Dublin City University, terminés récemment.

En 1964 les émigrés avaient trouvé un havre professionnel chez Robinson Keefe Devane. Ils décrivent Andrew Devane et Roddy McCaffrey comme « nos maîtres … qui ont fait preuve d'une si grande tolérance. » Alors qu'il serait tentant de faire le rapprochement entre la fusion du géométrique et du naturel dans leur œuvre et une influence durable de Wright chez RKD dans les années 60, ce cabinet a également donné aux jeunes polonais une base et un format pour analyser la réalité professionnelle locale. En effet on remarque chez les Wejchert – cabinet ouvert en 1974 après la réalisation d'éléments clefs de Belfield: Arts Block, banque et bâtiment administratif, que non seulement ils testent de nouveaux styles et idées mais mettent en application ces propositions. Le seul autre architecte immigré australien aux aspirations similaires – Raymond McGrath, n'a pas remporté le même succès.

Avec leur équipe de cinq associés, Andrzej et Danuta Wejchert continuent à faire face au monde capricieux des concours, en Irlande comme à l'étranger. Tout récemment ils ont proposé, pour les quais de Waterford, un ensemble de vecteurs inclinés séparant l'environnement construit de celui qui reste vierge: « traitant la rivière en grand salon' avec un espace culturel vitré 'comme un écran géant de TV ». Aucun autre cabinet d'architecture n'a participé à un si grand nombre de concours internationaux, allant de celui pour l'Organisation Internationale de Vienne et du Centre de Conférence en 1969 (des formes comme des totems abritant des terrasses superposées les unes au-dessus des autres) à celui d'une nouvelle université en Calabre, Italie. Pour cette université ils ont imaginé une superstructure cartésienne de salles de classe au-dessus d'un terrain vallonné occupé par des espaces communs – une coexistence exemplaire du rationalisme et du naturel.

Ils ont aussi participé à plusieurs reprises aux concours d'idées de Shinkenchiku au Japon. Le premier projet était celui d'une tour en trois sections avec trois boules suspendues au-dessus de la Méditerranée (envisagé pour le maestro Herbert von Karajan). Il y a eu ensuite un Musée du 20ème siècle ou des boîtes transparentes -chacune contenant des pièces appartenant à une décennie – s'élevaient à cheval au-dessus d'une ligne du temps chronologique mais fluide où on pouvait facilement suivre les principaux thèmes historiques tels des allées dans un jardin. Dans le bureau actuel à Baggot Street on peut voir les dessins, les maquettes de nombreux concours conservés comme des talismans, peut-être, ou des déclencheurs d'idées pour le développement du concept de futurs projets. Dans un autre ordre, le Centre des Visiteurs de la Grotte Aillwee a influencé les projets pour la montagne de Hong Kong en 1983 avec un ziggourat à demi enterré et évidé, adossé à la colline, caché derrière des bandes striées de jardinières.

Dans les années 1990, les Wejchert sont repartis construire en Pologne. Le Palais Sobanski est situé sur le Aleje Ujazdoskie, la partie du boulevard qui relie le Palais Royal dans la Vieille Ville de Varsovie au Palais d'été du Siècle des lumières à Wilanow à une dizaine de kilomètres au sud. C'est une voie prestigieuse ressemblant au Royal Mile d'Edimbourg et au grand axe cartésien qu'est la ligne droite qui va du Louvre, en traversant le quartier actuel de La Défense, aux propriétés de Louis XIV à l'ouest de Paris. Le Palais a ses propres caractéristiques françaises à savoir une composition symétrique avec des pavillons jumeaux et des jardins à la française. Actuellement occupé par un club privé, le bâtiment a été élégamment rénové. Les Wejchert ont creusé dans la cave et les parties avoisinantes pour laisser pénétrer la lumière naturelle et pour illuminer les niveaux les plus bas occupés par les cuisines et services au sous-sol du palais.

Sur l'un des côtés du Palais, mitoyen avec le mur de l'Ambassade de Grande Bretagne, le cabinet a également construit un pavillon de trois étages, en prisme, perpendiculaire au boulevard. Ses façades extérieures sont en verre, protégées des rayons bas du soleil par des persiennes composées de lames horizontales en verre. Leur projet polonais le plus récent est celui du Centre de Communication au sud du Palais Sobanski en se dirigeant vers Wilanow. Combinant des studios de TV, des espaces de distribution de vidéos et les bureaux d'une société d'internet à l'intérieur d'un cube relié par des marches, les façades sont en verre comme celles du pavillon du Palais Sobanski. Par contre le Centre est beaucoup plus grand et comprend deux vestibules remplis de lumière, l'un occupant un étage entier au-dessus de l'autre et tous deux coiffés d'un vaste dôme en verre. La géométrie est ici au service de l'agrément, les vestibules sont bordés de grandes fenêtres coulissantes permettant une vue large et laissant entrer de la lumière dans tout le bâtiment.

Certaines des démarches du cabinet des Wejchert s'assimileraient aux techniques de l'architecte hollandais Hermann Hertberger. Les écoles de Ballincollig et Ballynanty aux modules de polyester renforcé de verre, fabriquées dans les années 70 par un constructeur de bateau sur l'île de Wight et arrivant comme un cirque ambulant, sont arrangées en fragments circulaires où les éléments clos et les espaces intermédiaires unissent leur force dans un but commun. Des spécialistes hollandais en structures à savoir Hertzberger et, auparavant, Aldo van Eyck ont divisé les plans architecturaux en 'organigrammes', en disposant des activités cognitives séparées entre elles par des espaces d'activités partagées (activités ludiques pour enfants, rencontres informelles pour les adultes). Le Centre de Communication est, dans cette optique, tel une ruche de cristal attendant d'être animée par de multiples styles d'activités quotidiennes.

Le Helix à DCU lui ressemble, avec un ensemble de salles de spectacle fermées et séparées, se superposant, à un alignement de pièces plus conventionnelles en arrière-plan. Au niveau du sol, il offre plusieurs interprétations possibles du foyer aux formes courbes, qui peut être considéré comme vide – un espace en trop entre les trois espaces concaves – ou solide – comme une perspective verticale, pivot du complexe dans son ensemble. Avec, à la hauteur du toit, un cube lumineux bleu qui saillit sur un côté du bâtiment, l'Helix est une sorte de panneau d'affichage aux multiples faces s'offrant à la vue du campus et des passants sur Collins Avenue. Avec ses formes arrondies suggérant mouvement et accueil, le Helix est un exercice en composition géométrique, une manifestation supplémentaire de la recherche par le mouvement Moderne de la lumière et de la forme, travaillant au cœur des aléas de la réalité irlandaise.

——

Buildings & Projects

Buildings and Projects

4 – A Place to Work

5 – A Place to Live

6 – A Place for Leisure

7 – A Place for Culture and Spirituality

____

1 – A Place for Study

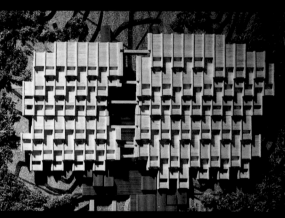

Second Level School
Brookfield, Co Dublin (1985)   52

Scoil Íde
Finglas, Dublin 11 (1986)

Primary School
Blessington, Co Wicklow (1987)

Robert Schuman Building
University of Limerick (1991)   57

Aeronautical and Environmental Technology Building
University of Limerick (1997)   60

Student Centre
University College Cork (1996)   62

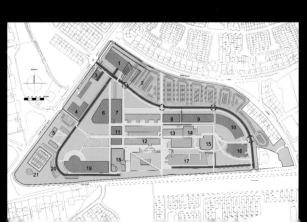

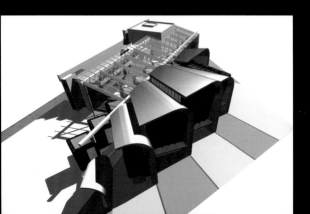

1 – A Place for Study

In parallel with the search for optimal organisation of study and research space, we endeavour to improve the environment of that space. For example, in the Dalkey School Project we introduced 'shared areas' instead of standard classrooms, allowing two classes to participate in group activities, thus expanding and enriching the curriculum offered to children.

To cope with the ubiquitous problem of light reflecting on computer screens at the WIT Information Technology Building, a special translucent wall admits natural light, eliminating reflections.

The airy atrium at the entry to the Nurse Education Building at WIT, allows an organisation of space that can be readily understood by the constant influx of new students. Thus, an easy flow is generated between staff rooms, laboratories, lecture rooms and social areas.

Dalkey School Project (1984)

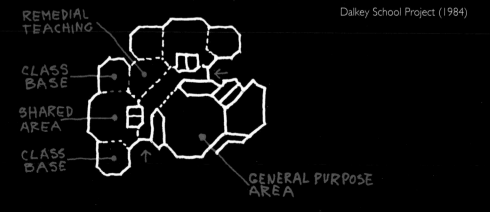

REMEDIAL
TEACHING

CLASS
BASE

SHARED
AREA

CLASS
BASE

GENERAL PURPOSE
AREA

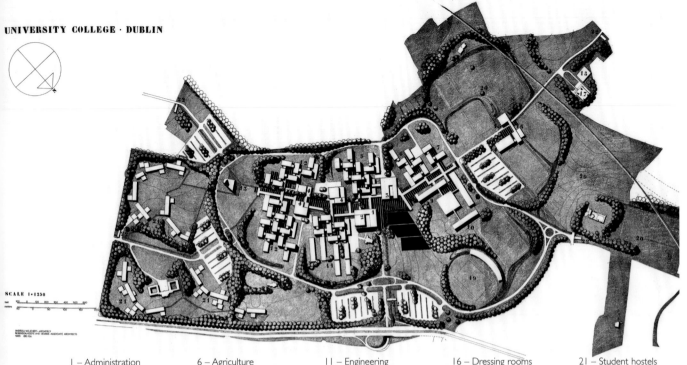

SCALE 1÷1250

1 – Administration
2 – Aula Maxima
3 – Library
4 – Student facilities
5 – Arts

6 – Agriculture
7 – Architecture
8 – Biology
9 – Chemistry
10 – Physics

11 – Engineering
12 – Medicine
13 – Church
14 – Swimming pool
15 – Gymnasium

16 – Dressing rooms
17 – Boiler house
18 – Maintenance building
19 – Stadium
20 – Playing fields

21 – Student hostels
22 – Gate lodges

Master Plan
University College Dublin

This design won the international architectural competition for an overall plan for the Belfield campus and the design for the Arts, Administration and Aula Maxima buildings. As long ago as 1949 it was decided to move University College Dublin from its overcrowded buildings to a new 300-acre site at Belfield, four miles south of its original location in the centre of Dublin. The international assessors' report described the various buildings in this submission as being 'arranged at either side of the pedestrian mall of interesting and irregular shape. The proposed development of the buildings for the various facilities on both sides of the partially covered pedestrian mall allows for a logical succession of the buildings required, whilst leaving between them views of courtyard and landscapes.'

The plan conceives a linear development of the campus, linking the buildings together by covered walkways, which become the lifeline of the campus. The buildings are sited as close as reasonably possible to each other in order to maintain walking distance of approximately six minutes (500m) between the two ends of the pedestrian mall. The close siting also helps to limit the underground service runs and roadworks. A ring road encircles the campus core, which is totally pedestrianised. The unity and homogeneous character of the campus during its development – which is phased over twenty years – depends on the scale of external finishes, consisting of varieties of concrete and, above all, on extensive landscaping. The Belfield campus now has 18,000 students and it is still growing.

design-completion – 1963-1964
area – 150ha approx
client – University College Dublin

Master plan

Covered walkways along pedestrian wall

Model

opposite – Aerial view showing first phase, consisting of Administration Building, Arts / Commerce, Library, Restaurant and Sciences

APPRAISAL – UNIVERSITY COLLEGE AT DUBLIN
by Lance Wright

How well will this university look, as a university in, say, fifty years? The answer to this question seems to depend more on the long-term assessment of works of the modern movement than on particular design skills.

But there are points to notice about this design which suggest that it may weather better in popular esteem than most of the new universities in these islands. We have already remarked on Andrzej Wejchert's responsiveness to the physical climate, as expressed in his extraordinary exertions in the matter of planting. This was wise. Because (for excellent reasons) good modern buildings represent bold statements unaccompanied by small talk, they stand in great need of planting. But he also showed himself responsive to the Irish social and economic climates. His aim all along has been not to build anything which would not go well with Ireland. He took the view that his university must reflect the sort of building which will be general in the country during the foreseeable future. This prompted his choice of precast concrete as the finishing material (Ireland, we must remember, is not rich in clays), and, as a foil to the prevailing green, to fix on a very white aggregate; this too prompted him to reject Sir Basil Spence's proposal to face the library in Portland stone.

The idea that a university should fit in with the prevailing social and architectural scenes was far from being an obvious one to the university designers of the 1960s, for this was still the period of the heartless revolutionary gesture. Conceived in an age of heroic, thundering architectural miscalculations, Belfield must be chalked up as representing a good workable idea, sensitively carried out. It stands a decent chance of looking better, and thus of rising in the unconscious esteem of its users at a time when so many other buildings in the same class, built at the same time, are looking worse.

Excerpt from 'Appraisal – University College at Dublin', *The Architects' Journal* (London), °157, April 1973, pp.857-78. Lance Wright was an editor of *The Architectural Review* and *The Architects' Journal*.

Administration Building
University College Dublin

OPENING OF ADMINISTRATION BUILDING, UCD
by Dr JJ Hogan

Returning to the splendid building we are inaugurating today. If it in any way springs from anything in Earlsfort Terrace, it is not from the actual offices there, but rather from the Great Hall as it was for some weeks every autumn, with office tables ranged along the walls, and students coming to the appropriate point for information, or to register or pay fees. This building is part of the tripartite group, Arts/Commerce/Law, Administration and Aula Maxima, which is in Mr Wejchert's charge. I greatly admire both of the sections he has completed, but to my mind this one [Administration Building] — bold, simple, unified — is perhaps the finer. On behalf of the College, I thank Mr Wejchert and all those who worked with him, and the contractors, Messrs Sisk and their staff, who have done so much work for us, soundly, smooth-ly, and according to timetable.

When I think of Mr Wejchert, my mind often wanders into speculation on human affairs and the strange chances and coincidences through which they may arrive at a pattern. By

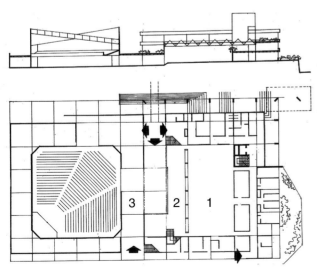

1 – General office hall / 2 – Public concourse / 3 – Aula Maxima

1955 University College had acquired most of its land We had a layout plan, we were ready to build, and the urgency of our doing so was great and was well recognised. Mr Wejchert was then still at school or, at most, beginning the study of architecture. Of this young man, and of the buildings of University College Dublin, it might then have been said: 'Alien they seemed to be / No mortal eye could see / The intimate welding of their later history'.

But our building projects were held back, with the single exception of the Science Block, until we could have the result of an international architectural competition, opened in August 1963. By then, Mr Wejchert was just old enough to compete, but it was still necessary, to allow of his becoming the chief figure in the building of our College, that ... he should win it. He has been eight years in a country which must have been very strange to him when he came here, and he has written his name indelibly on the history of our institution.

I have taken you some distance back in the history of our transfer to Belfield. If you will allow me a few moments more, I shall go a little further back. My own first interest in long-term College planning was formed when, in 1944, the late Dr Conway set up the Statutory Officers' Committee. It studied the whole matter very fully and recommended for the College buildings far more extensive than we then possessed, though much smaller than those we now have and project. Dr Michael Tierney devoted a great part of his effort, through the seventeen years of his presidency, to the new College. Under him the decision was taken that it should be at Belfield, and at the end of those seventeen years he saw the Science Building almost complete, and in the summer of 1964 handed to Mr Wejchert the prize in the international competition which made him the architect of these buildings and supervisor of the whole scheme. I hope that Dr Tierney will be present as a visitor and well-wisher at the opening of several more College buildings, and it would give me very great pleasure if I might join with him – *fortunati ambo* – in the same capacity on such occasions. I now declare open the Administration Building of University College Dublin.

excerpt from a speech by the President of UCD, Dr JJ Hogan, at the opening of the Administration Building, 14 April 1972

RIAI GOLD MEDAL 1971-1973

Citation – *This is a building of great character and strength. It takes full advantage of a worthy setting, and balances in harmony with other fine buildings which are part of its environment. With the directness of a form constructed in concrete, it combines the sensitivity of fine detail and finish.*

The approaches both from the open air and though the transparent first-floor link from the Arts Block provoke a dramatic

interest in what lies beyond. The floor levels and vertical circulation are cleverly related to a contoured site.

The space created by the large central office and concourse adds warmth and cheerfulness to dignity and elegance. The rest of the accommodation is simply and directly related to the dominant central space. Again, crisp, subtle detail enhances the atmosphere of relaxed efficiency. The building has the special merit of appearing complete and yet embodying the flexibility to envisage and provide for very substantial future expansion. It is, in every aspect, a building of distinction.

Views of pedestrian bridge from Administration Building to Arts / Commerce

ARCHITECTS' DESCRIPTION

The building has a centralising function relating to the entire university campus. In addition to normal university administration, it is used by academic staff, students and visitors. The offices of the president, registrar, secretary and the governing body are located in this building, and it also serves as a distribution centre. Registration of all students takes place here.

The building features a dominant central space (see plan on

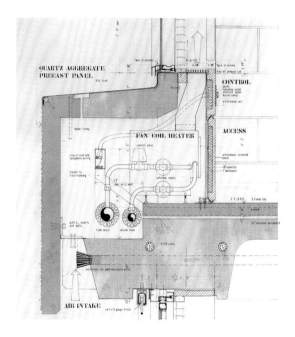

page 37): the general office hall (1) and the public concourse (2). Cellular accommodation is simply and directly related to this space. Future planning includes an extension to this building for the Aula Maxima (3).

address – Belfield, Dublin 4
design-completion – 1963-1972
area – 5,500m²
client – University College Dublin
awards – RIAI Triennial Gold Medal 1971-1973

---

above – Detail of perimeter services, a key detail to the entire complex
right – General office

Arts / Commerce Building
University College Dublin

This building is planned for 5,000 students and 300 staff. It consists of adaptable, standard teaching units of various heights, grouped around inner courtyards and inter-connected with service/circulation towers. The lower two floors contain eleven lecture theatres for 150, 200, 300 and 500 students. The first floor contains 48 general classrooms from 24 to 100 seats for the use of all departments. Upper floors have teaching and research areas allocated to various departments. This building is directly connected to the Administration Building and the library by two enclosed bridge walkways. The basic structure is prestressed reinforced concrete, with prefabricated concrete horizontal cladding and in-situ concrete service towers. Mechanical services are distributed horizontally through peripheral ducts. The organised relationships between function, structure and services is clearly expressed throughout the building both internally and externally.

address – Belfield, Dublin 4
design-completion – 1963-1970
area – 27,000m²
client – University College Dublin

---

left – Courtyard

below – Projection showing proposed expansion

opposite – View from pedestrian wall

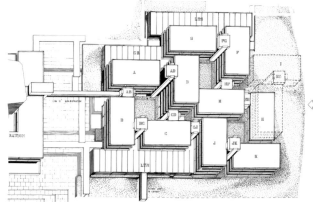

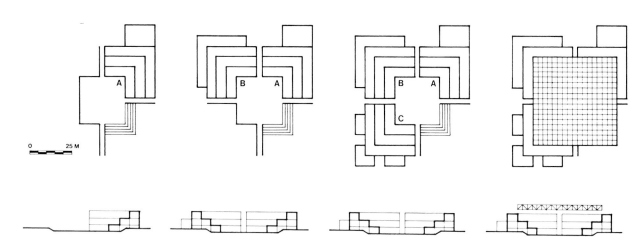

BLOCK A contains Administration Building, service facilities, club rooms and bars.

BLOCK B provides subdividable assembly areas, a theatre/Student Union chamber, workshops and dressing rooms, and society rooms and offices.

BLOCK C increases accommodation for societies and clubs, and, in addition, includes common rooms and facilities for leisure facilities.

A space frame with a transparent roof creates a covered forum for meetings, exhibitions, shows and concerts, viewed from the terraces of the surrounding blocks.

Students' Union Building
University College Dublin

The project was based on a phased development of general students' facilities, depending on funds being available. The proposed solution consisted of a building type which could be divided into parts, each built at a different time and in the preferred sequence. The building form provided for stepped structures where the roofs would be used as terraces, forming a large amphitheatre. The final phase of development envisaged a translucent roof over a forum and terraces, which would give a unique semi-enclosed space that could be used as a gathering place of social and cultural importance for the whole campus.

address – Belfield, Dublin 4
design – 1978
area – 5,000m²
client – University College Dublin.

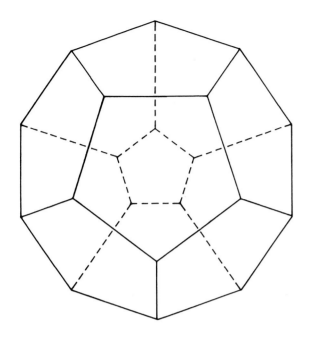

Water Tower
University College Dublin

The tower was built to provide constant water pressure for all campus buildings. The pentagonal stem is of reinforced concrete constructed in one continuous pour, utilising a sliding shutter. The tank, made of waterproof reinforced concrete, is in the form of a duodecahedron.

address – Belfield, Dublin 4
design-completion – 1971-1972
height – 60m
capacity – 150, 000 gallons / 700,000 litres
client – University College Dublin
awards – Irish Concrete Society Award, 1979

45

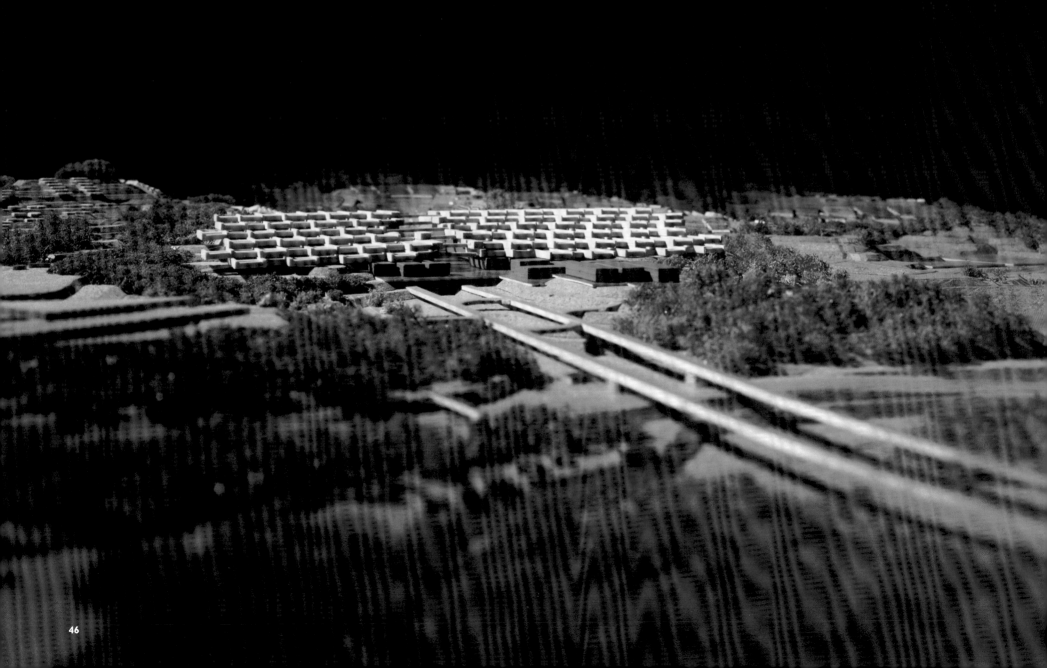

Universita degli Studi della Calabria – Competition

This competition involved the site layout for a campus accommodating 12,000 students, and a detailed design of the first phase for 4,000 students.

The project focused on a high degree of flexibility towards future growth in didactic and research areas. The departmental buildings are standardised dimensionally. They are designed as a multi-layered bridge over the valley. Social and cultural buildings are located along the valley – easily accessible to students and to the adjoining community.

The student residences are integrated with the existing villages on surrounding hillsides.

address – Cosenza, Italy
design – 1973
areas of Phase 1 development: departments – 54,000m²;
    cultural/social – 43,000m²; *student residences* – 95,000m²

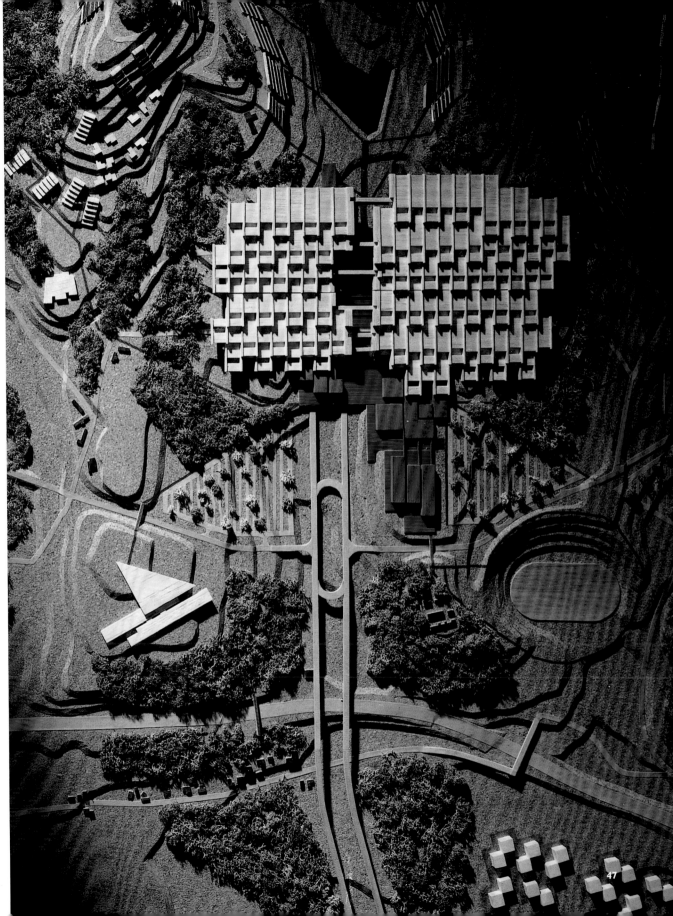

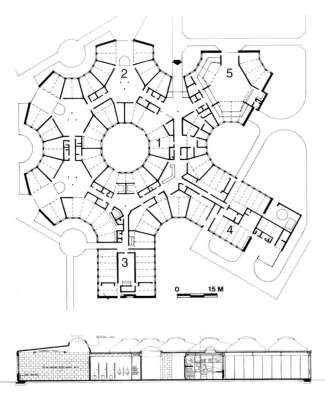

Ballincollig Community School

This school for 810 pupils is organised around a main closed-circuit circulation. The layout provides a high degree of connectivity, and distinguishes between areas of common interest and those for more specific functions. The inner ring contains the humanities departments (1), while the outer branches are for 'base units' (2), sciences (3), practical arts (4), and multifunctional areas (5). The social area within the 'base unit' can be combined with adjoining classrooms. A key role is played by the movable resource module, which distributes teaching aids and acts as a space divider. The structure consists of structural GRP (glass-reinforced polyester) single-skin roof and wall panels. A second, identical school building was erected in Ballynanty, Co Limerick.

address – Ballincollig, Co Cork
design-completion – 1974-1976
area – 4,800m²
client – Department of Education

Dalkey School Project

The school is composed of two parts – an L-shaped classroom block and a general-purpose area with outdoor teaching and playing terrace over. The classroom block is directed towards open fields. The assembly area and terrace face south-west to the road.

Because of the site limitations, the school was designed partially as a two-storey building with two groups of shared areas on the ground floor and two groups on the first floor. Each group is composed of two class bases with shared area and toilet block. A remedial teaching room on the ground floor can be used separately or as a joint element between both groups if required.

The general-purpose area, embraced by the classroom wings, is located a few steps below ground-floor level. If required, it can take advantage of the adjoining circulation and the remedial teaching room to create a 'stage' for plays or for major assemblies.

address – Dalkey, Co Dublin
design-completion – 1980-1984
area – 1,050m²
client – Educate Together, Glenageary, Co Dublin

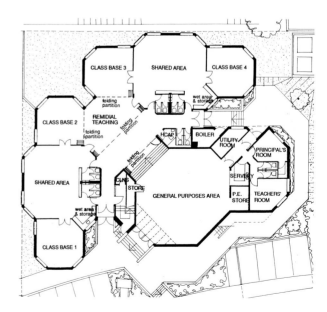

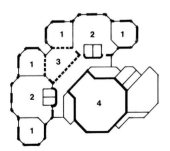

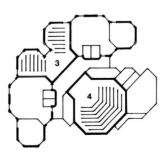

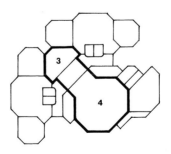

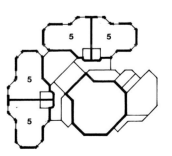

This eight-class primary school is based on the shared-area teaching method. This experimental project uses shared-area classrooms for children of two different age groups. The diagram explains how two class bases (1) are joined by one shared area (2).

Here two class bases are connected to the remedial teaching room (3) and create an alternative assembly area to the general-purpose area (4).

The general-purpose area (4) can be enlarged by the inclusion of circulation and the remedial teaching room (3) for meetings, plays and shows.

The school can also revert to the traditional teaching method, where the base unit is increased by half of the shared area, thus becoming a full-sized self-contained classroom (5). With all this flexibility, the school becomes a working tool in the hands of an imaginative teacher.

Second Level School, Brookfield

This school, for 1,000 pupils, is designed in four main functional blocks. The blocks are connected by a linear circulation spine, which, in some parts, is two storeys high and lit by central roof lights.

Laboratories and workshops are located on the ground floor, with all classrooms on the first floor, forming a semi-circle directed towards mountain views to the south. The first-floor plan is narrower than the deep ground-floor plan, providing all areas below with well-diffused natural light admitted through the windows and rooflights. The structure of the building consists of a reinforced concrete frame. The external walls are constructed of prefabricated GRC (glass-reinforced cement) and insulated window panels.

address – Tallaght, Co Dublin
design-completion – 1982-1985
area – 6,000m²
client – Department of Education

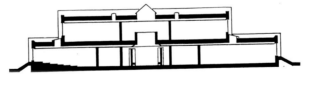

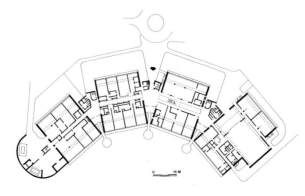

AnCo Training Centre

Large-volume training areas (1) with service and delivery yards and car parks are located in the western part of the site, adjoining the public road. Small-volume training (2), training and social administrative areas (3) and service areas (4) are stepped down towards the park and housing to the east. These elements are inter-connected by the internal route (5), which acts as a distribution system for trainees, personnel, goods and all major piped services from the boiler house.

address – Loughlinstown, Co Dublin
design-completion – 1980-1983
area – 7,500m^2
client – AnCo, the Industrial Training Authority
awards – *Sunday Independent* Arts Award for 'outstanding achievement for industrial architecture', 1983
    – An Taisce Context Award, 1984
    – *Plan* Building of the Year Award, 1984
    – National Rehabilitation Board Building Design Awards, 1983-84, New Building category (commendation)

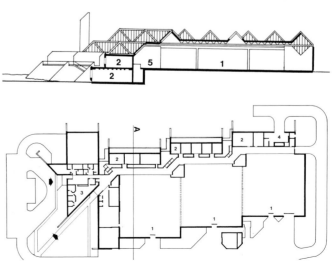

JOB TRAINING CENTRE COMBINES STRENGTH AND NEIGHBOURLINESS
by Donald Canty

Approximately half the total population of Ireland is 25 years old, or younger. The Irish government puts high priority on training the young for what jobs there are on the market.

The AnCo Centre in the Dublin suburb of Loughlinstown was built last year for the industrial training authority as part of this effort. Designed by A&D Wejchert Architects, it is a sizable facility, serving some 800 trainees, plus staff, on a typical day. Yet it was built on a narrow six-acre site that had been a walled orchard between two small-scale housing developments.

This context, and fire codes, required that the Centre keep a low profile. It is essentially a linear, one-storey building, but a 30ft drop in the site permitted insertion of extra space on the lower side. Along this side are strung classrooms, small-scale training spaces, and miscellaneous communal and administrative rooms. Aligned behind them, in the body of the building, are three very large (130ft clear span) training spaces. They, and the smaller rooms, open onto and are separated from each other by a wide corridor that serves as a pedestrian 'street'. This circulation spine avoids penetration of any of the other interior spaces. It culminates at an angular projection that houses offices, a greenhouse entry, and, on the lower level, the dining hall.

Striping the building's roof are thirteen long skylights. They are pyramidal in section, so that where their ends protrude they reflect the peaked roofs of the neighbouring houses. The skylights give the interiors a bright and cheerful character. They also result in some heat gain, but more often than not this is welcome in Ireland's cool, damp climate. The cheerfulness is enhanced by an almost exuberant use of colour inside. Among the colours is a variety of greens, as might be expected, including an especially pleasing dark one that is used on the steel framing, inside and out. The colourful metal surfaces contrast with unadorned grey masonry interior walls.

The big spaces – and the huge, factory-type doors leading into them from the upper driveway – were scaled to serve training in the use of large industrial equipment. However, in the less than two years since completion, the pendulum of employment opportunities has swung so strongly from heavy equipment to computers that some of the big spaces have been partitioned into cubicles for computer training. Partitioning has cut them up, but it also has proved the building's flexibility.

Exterior walls are of prefabricated lightweight panels of glass-reinforced cement, incorporating polystyrene-bead aggregated concrete insulation and finished with exposed coarse sand. They have softly rounded edges (to emphasise that they are made of a plastic material, according to Martin Carey, project architect). 'Concrete', Carey points out, is 'Ireland's only truly indigenous material.' The rocky island, he notes, 'has plenty of limestone and cement'.

———
from *Architecture* (New York), Sept 1984, pp.197-98. Donald Canty, was editor of *Architecture*, the magazine of the American Institute of Architects.

———

ANCO TRAINING CENTRE

View of foyer

Robert Schuman Building
University of Limerick

This three-storey, brick-clad building accommodates computer science, information systems and educational departments for 1,000 students. It terminates the central composition of the International Business Centre, which was planned around an ornamental lake, making a very strong statement on the campus by establishing its western boundary. Most of the accommodation consists of 24-to-100-seat classrooms, reading rooms, computer rooms and staff rooms.

At the centre, where the planning axis meets the building, the interior has been opened up by eliminating all brick elements and introducing a stepped glazed curtain wall. This part of the building accommodates the main entrance and reception at ground-floor level, a coffee shop at first-floor level, and communal/social areas at second-floor level. Because of the stepped section, the space gets larger as it moves up through the building. The open quality of this central space is further emphasised by the introduction of a gently curved roof which oversails the flat roofs of the adjoining blocks.

address – Plassey, Limerick
design-completion – 1986-1991
area – 4300m²
client – University of Limerick

right – Students' social area
below – Plan
overleaf – Sculpture by Alexandra Wejchert: *Phoenix*, 1991, stainless steel

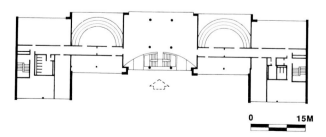

0   15M

ROBERT SCHUMAN BUILDING

Aeronautical and Environmental Technology Building
University of Limerick

This is the first stage of a multi-phased development which will accommodate scientific research functions of various types. The building consists of research laboratories, seminar rooms and staff rooms for aeronautical and environmental technology. A covered pedestrian bridge connects the building with the core campus buildings.

The design philosophy and architectural treatment of the building is disciplined and ordered to reflect the most up-to-date nature of scientific research.

The materials used are similar to those in the adjacent buildings – a deliberate decision which continues the college's development in a harmonious manner. The scale, use and detailing of these materials has been carefully reinterpreted to reflect the philosophy stated above, while still remaining in sympathy with the existing buildings.

address – Plassey, Limerick
design-completion – 1995-1997
area – 3,700m²
client – University of Limerick

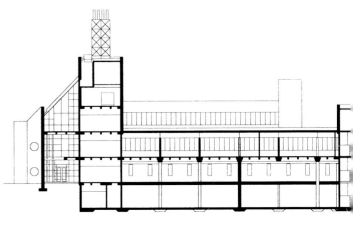

Glazed pedestrian bridge

opposite

Multistorey concourse

Cross-section through concourse and laboratories

Student Centre
University College Cork

The Student Centre provides a social focus and communal facilities for college students. It is built of brick and local white limestone, and faces the River Lee. The larger spaces – common room and lounge/bar – are on the first floor overlooking the river valley. In the adjoining walled garden, a glazed pergola and landscaped terraces with seating extend the various facilities.

address – Western Road, Cork
design-completion – 1993-1996
area – 2,900m²
client – University College Cork

Level 1

Level 2

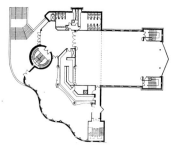

Level 3

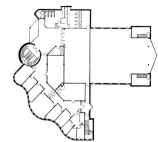

Plans
View from lower grounds
opposite – Common room

STUDENT CENTRE, UCC

Main stairs
Students' bar

opposite
Glazed pergola
Cork white limestone detail
Glazing detail

O'Rahilly Building
University College Cork

This building creates a major new square with the adjoining Boole Library, Honan Chapel and Student Centre. With regard to the sensitive nature of the site, as well as the historic environment of the campus, the building's design was developed to reduce its scale by the introduction of stepping, by a creative mix of materials with fenestration in sympathy with the adjoining buildings, and by the selective use of Cork white limestone, which is used on major public buildings in Cork and on the campus.

Cork white limestone has been used extensively in the external elevation of this building in two ways: random stone work on the heavy base, salvaged from the demolished Honan Hostel, and dressed ashlar, which was quarried in east Cork. The structure of the building is reinforced concrete columns supporting single-span, pre-stressed, post-tension flat slab, which spans 11.7 metres. This gives a very flexible structure and free interior, well suited to various academic functions.

address – Western Road, Cork
design-completion – 1995-2000
area – 2,500m²
client – University College Cork

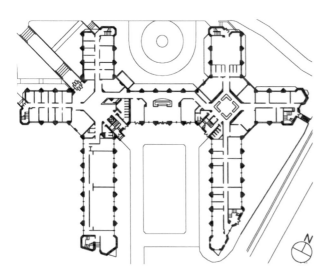

1 – Quadrangle
2 – Boole Library
3 – O'Rahilly Building
4 – Student Centre

Luke Wadding Library
Waterford Institute of Technology

The user requirements as set out in the brief included:
- flexibility
- computer technology compatibility
- user-comfortable environment
- energy-efficiency (i.e. a 'green' building)
- progressive image
- clearly defined circulation and control.

Based on the site conditions and brief requirements, a multi-layered approach to the building was developed. As with any public building, clearly defined circulation routes with reference points for ease of orientation are crucial. A strong 'spine' running the length of the building clearly defines circulation. In keeping with the history of large-volume reader spaces, multistorey atria are provided. These act as focal spaces from which users can orientate themselves within the building.

The main reading space is arranged in a multistorey atrium facing north, while smaller spaces are designated for seminar, staff and store rooms. The building is designed as a 'green building' for maximum energy-efficiency.

The use of passive environmental control is a strong theme within the building, and is one of the generating forces behind the linear nature of the building, which maximises natural light and ventilation. The image and expression of the building further stress this point. The south wall of the building, facing the Cork Road, has been designed as a heavy masonry wall to minimise traffic-noise disruption in the user space. It has small strip windows with external brise-soleil to minimise solar heat-gain without compromising natural lighting. The north, sloped façade is generously glazed to admit dispersed light to the large atrium volume. The whole structure is exposed to provide a thermal mass to minimise temperature fluctuations within the building. This is further enhanced by using the ventilation system at night to cool the structure to counteract peak daytime heat loads.

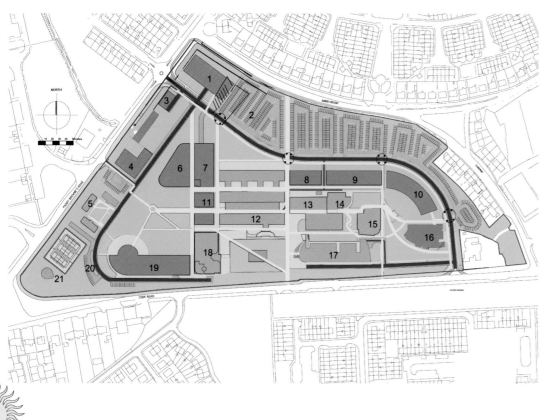

1 – Multistorey car park
2 – Car-parking
3 – Waste-recycling
4 – Creche (1,000m² / single storey)
5 – Student residences
6 – Built environment (5,000m² / 2-3 storey)
7 – Engineering (3,000m² / 2-3 storey)
8 – Business School (8,000m² / 4 storey)
9 – Business School
10 – Future building (possible Nurse
      Education Building 1,850m² extension)
11 – Student services (3,000m² / 3 storey)
12 – 1969 building
13 – 1977 building
14 – Canteen (864m² / 2 storey)
15 – IT Building (884m² / 2 storey)
16 – Nursing School (3,760m² / 3 storey)
17 – Library Building
18 – Existing Sports Building
19 – Future School of Tourism and Leisure
      (7,660m² / 3 storey)
20 – Future visitor parking
21 – Location for major sculpture

below (bottom to top) – Ground, 1st and 2nd floor plans

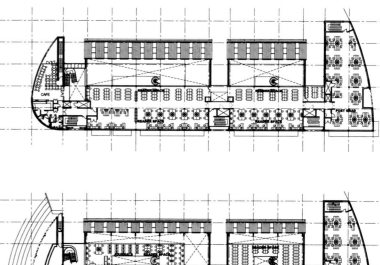

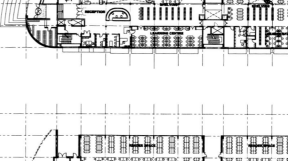

Roof profile to create negative pressure to
aid air exhaustion

Back-up mechanical extract system

Air exhausted through automatically
controlled opening glazing linked to BMS

Rooflights to maximise use of
north light

Percentage of glazing to achieve
optimum balance between heat-
loss, heat-gain and daylighting

brise-soleil on south façade

Localised opening sections

South façade, roof and cellular spaces
placed on south side of building act as
shield from heat-gain, noise and pollution

ROAD

THERMAL INERTIA (FREE COOLING) ENVIRONMENTAL SYSTEM
• air supply by displacement ventilation through raised floor plenum
• mechanical extract at high level
• exposed structural mass as heating/cooling reservoir
• night ventilation used to reduce quantity of stored heat in the thermal mass and flush out the building,
  thus proving a heat-sink for daytime heat-gains and increasing potential radioactive heat-loss from people
• provide air movement and comfort conditioning

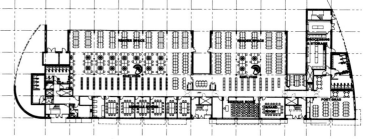

The selection of furniture has been treated as a continuation of the design to ensure a well co-ordinated and complete building. The building has been designed in as compact a form as possible, which incorporates deep multistorey spaces. All equipment purchased for the building is low-energy to minimise energy consumption and heat-generation. Insulation levels were set as high as budgets would allow. All glazing and external wall elements are double-sealed to a high standard.

address – Cork Road, Waterford
design-completion – 1997-2000
area – 5,500m²
client – Waterford Institute of Technology
awards – Department of the Environment Sustainable
　　　Building Award, 2000
　　　– Opus Building of the Year Award, 2000 (commended)

LUKE WADDING LIBRARY, WIT
by Ted Lynch

The Luke Wadding building articulates the library's eternal mission to facilitate expression and understanding of acquired knowledge. It reflects the actuality that ICT (Information and Communication Technology) is a key component in any learning facility, and it reveals to the user the hybrid nature of modern academic libraries: traditional print materials and new technologies co-exist, and the design of the new library promotes an understanding of their complementarity and mutual enrichment. The success of the project means that the Institute's library service can develop a building with strategic value for WIT in the years ahead, enabling the Institute to meet a commitment to higher education for its society.

Excerpt from 'Future Direction', *Leabharlann Luke Wadding* (WIT, Waterford, 2002). Ted Lynch is WIT Librarian.

LUKE WADDING LIBRARY, WIT

Interior of multistorey reading room
opposite – Façade to city

Walton Information Technology Building
Waterford Institute of Technology

This information technology building accommodates eighteen large computer laboratories for teaching, and associated technical rooms and staff offices, all arranged around a three-storey roof-lit atrium. It is also the computer hub for the entire campus.

The building is unique in its control of natural light to provide glare-free, comfortable conditions for working at computers. The building is environmentally friendly and incorporates a number of sustainability concepts, which were developed by the design team in conjunction with the Energy Research Group, University College Dublin.

address – Cork Road, Waterford
design-completion dates – 2001-2004
area – 3,061 m²
client – Waterford Institute of Technology
awards – Opus Building of the Year Award, 2005
    (commended)

1. Atrium
2. Lift
3. Computer Laboratory
4. Roof Terrace

Student Restaurant
Waterford Institute of Technology

The number of students at Waterford Institute of Technology has dramatically increased over recent years. With this increase in numbers, there has been a commensurate increase in demand for catering facilities for the students.

The new restaurant, seating 425, is designed with accommodation at two levels within a single large two storey, south-facing volume. An overhanging roof controls solar heat-gain and shelters the extended pedestrian circulation spine. The restaurant expands out into the covered area during the warmer months of the year. The building has fully glazed walls facing the campus pedestrian spine and the Walton Building.

address – Cork Road, Waterford
design-completion –2003-2004
area – 2,500m²
client – Waterford Institute of Technology

opposite – Night-time view, with restaurant on left and Walton building on right

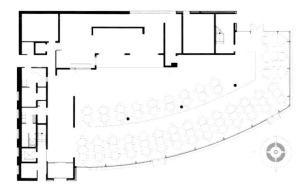

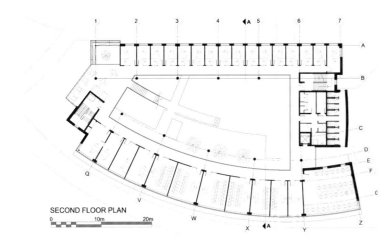

SECOND FLOOR PLAN

0   10m   20m

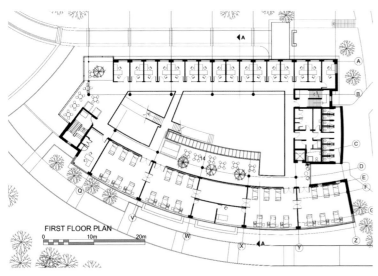

FIRST FLOOR PLAN

0   10m   20m

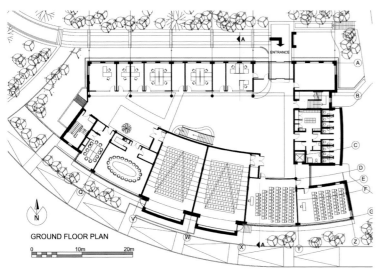

N

GROUND FLOOR PLAN

0   10m   20m

Nurse Education Building
Waterford Institute of Technology

The newly completed Nurse Education Building at Waterford Institute of Technology comprises 3,760m² over three storeys, with circulation and informal lounge spaces arranged around a generous top-lit atrium. This building forms part of a broader concept for accommodation for health sciences in third-level educational institutions in Ireland.

The spatial organisation of the building can be read clearly on entry to its airy, top-lit atrium: large classrooms, lecture theatres and laboratories are located to the south; smaller staff offices to the north; vertical circulation and toilets are located to the east; and social areas on all three levels look towards the campus at the west end.

The atrium becomes the focus and heart of the building. A curved central stair connects all three levels as they step outwards, allowing the atrium to widen towards the top providing more light at ground-floor level. The stepping within the atrium is reflected along the southern façade, where higher levels project outwards, minimising solar-gain to the levels below. The curved façade also draws the pedestrian route from the entrance area into the heart of the campus.

The external materials, which consist of white concrete brick, clear double-glazing and painted metalwork, reflect the materials used in other recently competed campus buildings, and consolidate the aesthetic unity of the Institute. Internally, particular attention was directed towards the use and detailing of timber. Because of its organic quality and warmth, it is used for built-in furniture, reception desk, benches, shelves, tables, and for joinery throughout the building.

Energy use – The Nurse Education Building is designed to consume only 50% of the energy

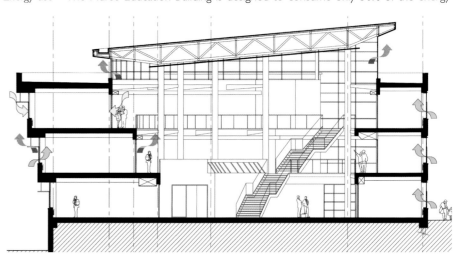

used by a similar building constructed to good practice standards. According to the energy readings for the building to date, these high standards have been achieved.

Form – The building's atrium is central to the environmental strategy, drawing air through deeper spaces, driving the night-cooling strategy, and filling the building with natural, glare-free daylight. Larger rooms which benefit from passive solar-gain are placed to the south, with smaller offices to the north. This clear passive solar strategy is matched with a distinctive shading strategy on the south façade that reduces summer gains.

Temperature control – The entire building is naturally ventilated with the exception of the toilets and lecture theatres. All teaching areas have exposed slab soffits, and rooms to the south are provided with motorised windows that are both locally controlled and form part of the BMS-implemented night-cooling strategy. The atrium vents are also opened as part of the night-cooling strategy, and draw air from deeper rooms through transfer vents. The south façade is stepped at each floor to offer natural shading during summer months, and this shading is supplemented by further shading below the motorised windows.

Lighting – Daylight factors exceed 5% in almost all rooms, which means that the artificial lighting can be turned off for 80% of the occupied period. In addition to the main façade glazing, glare-free daylight is drawn from the atrium into all rooms, including the rear of the lecture theatres, providing a constant contact with the external environment.

Structure – The building comprises three stories over basement with a design based on an elongated 'doughnut' configuration. The differing accommodation requirements imposed differing demands on the structural concept, which, in turn, led to a hybrid of in-situ concrete and steel structural frame.

Façade facing the Cork Road, with the Library building in the background

opposite – Plans and cross-section through atrium

OPUS BUILDING OF THE YEAR AWARD, 2006 –
HIGHLY COMMENDED

Citation – *The WIT campus continues to improve with this latest addition. The building's atrium is central to its use by students, but it is also central to its environmental strategy for daylighting, natural ventilation and energy consumption.*

address – Cork Road, Waterford
design-completion – 2003-2006
area – 3,760m²
client – Waterford Institute of Technology
awards – Opus Building of the Year Award, 2006
   (highly commended)
   – Dept of Environment, Heritage & Local Government,
   Best Sustainable Project, 2007
   – RIAI Irish Architecture Award, 2007

NURSE EDUCATION BUILDING, WIT

Details of seat in atrium, reception deck, restrooms

opposite – The atrium

Tourism and Leisure Education Building
Waterford Institute of Technology

The building provides a range of high-quality courses in catering, hospitality, leisure and tourism. The student will acquire a comprehensive education in hospitality and tourism.

The many different functions of the building are brought together in a linear form, which curves at its western end to express the informal public spaces. The building is expressed as a solid element, with glazed recesses punched out of the solid massing of the building to bring daylight into the deep plans. The large drum gives the building a strong presence on the site, as it is seen from the Cork Road.

address – Cork Road, Waterford
design-completion – 2000-2008
client – Waterford Institute of Technology

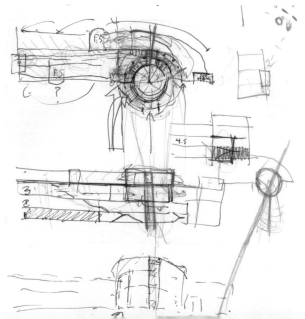

Youghal Community School

This school for 1,000 pupils is designed as a two storey building in order to limit travel distances between rooms. It is arranged as four wings radiating from the central, two-storey general-purpose area. The entrance to the school leads directly into this double-height volume, which is the focal point of the school both architecturally and functionally.

Each wing is distinguished by a different colour – blue, green or orange. Three wings accommodate teaching spaces, and the fourth a gymnasium. The three teaching wings contain deep spaces for practical use on the ground floor, and shallower classroom-type spaces on the upper floor to facilitate the use of rooflighting to the deeper ground-floor spaces.

The design is prepared in such a way as to maximise the use of natural lighting and ventilation. This has resulted in a bright and airy building which is pleasant to be in and that has an atmosphere conducive to learning.

address – Co Cork
design-completion – 2002-2006
area – 8,000m²
client – Department of Education & Science

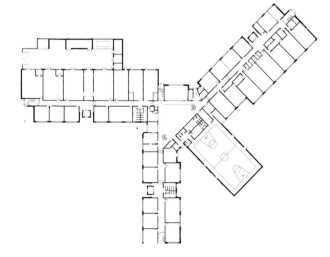

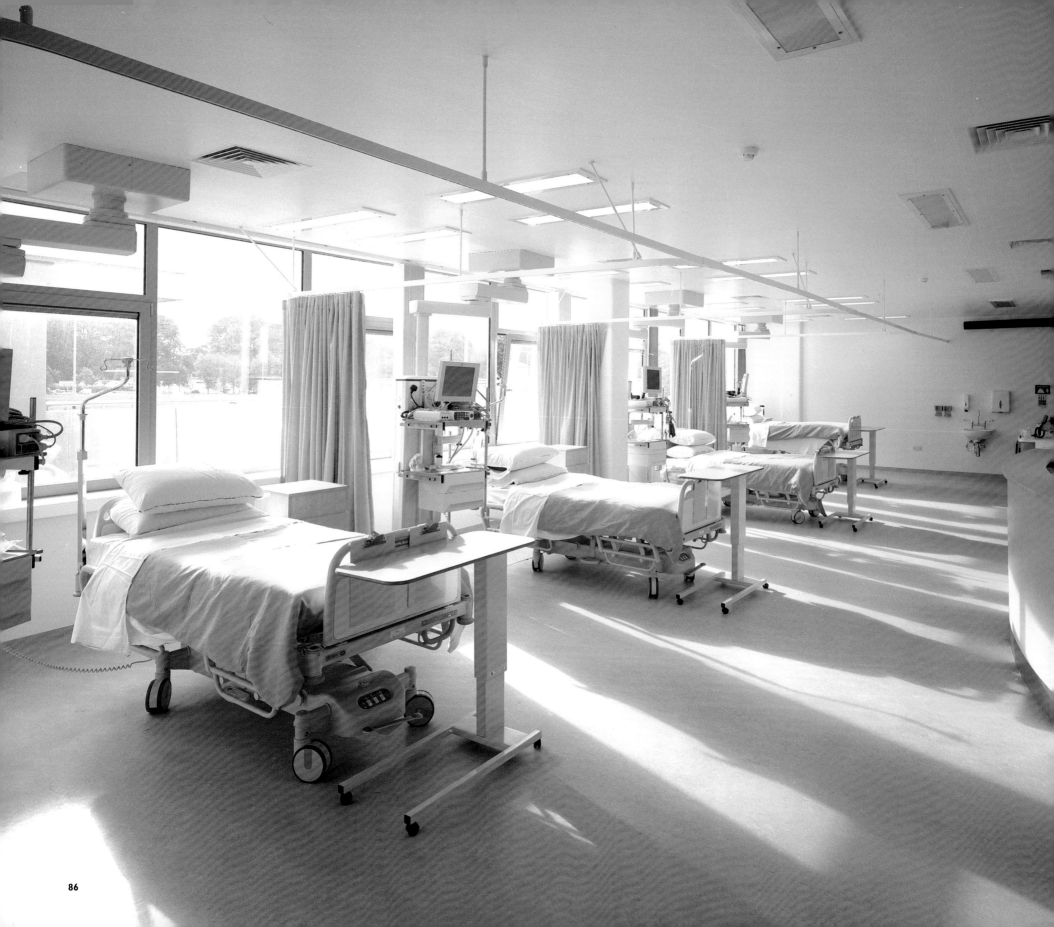

2 – A Place for Healing

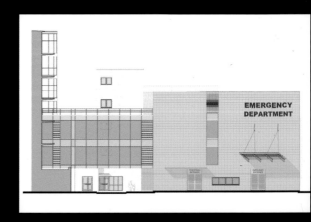

Mark's Lane Health Centre
Dublin 2 (2008)

Irishtown Health Centre
Dublin 4 (2008)   118

CRC/HSE Regional Assessment and Treatment Centre
Waterford (2009)

2 – A Place for Healing

Hospitals belong to a very special group of buildings which are the largest and most complex known to society. However, functionality and complexity should not prevent a hospital being pleasant to work in or having an atmosphere where people feel cared for. Nature, daylight, fresh air and tranquillity play an important role in the design of healing environments. Clinical evidence views nature, whether an enclosed courtyard or an internal garden, as beneficial to health. In the same way, natural daylight brings a feeling of normality to all – patients, staff and visitors.

Proposal for Children's Hospital (2007)

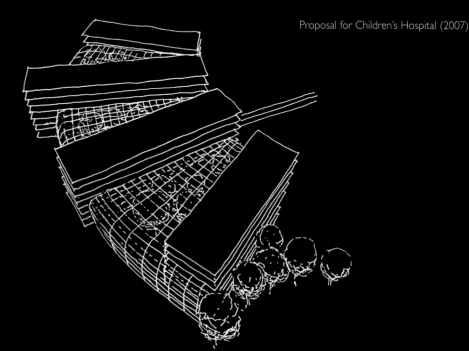

Designing for Health

DANUTA KORNAUS-WEJCHERT

The progress of modern medicine has produced profound changes in developed societies. Average lifetime is extended, the mortality rate as a result of diseases is decreasing. Treatment, medical equipment and surgical procedures have become more sophisticated and technology more advanced. The demand on hospital functionality has been reinforced by the provision of free-flow services, with artificial light and ventilation. Additionally, constant levels of temperature and the demand for a 'clean room' environment tends to produce an image of a high-tech laboratory, where sick patients could become even more worried and frightened.

Hospitals belong to a very special group of buildings which are the largest and most complex known to society. However, functionality and complexity should not prevent a hospital being pleasant to work in or having an atmosphere where people feel cared for. A hospital can also be warm and friendly. As an example, a lot of waiting takes place in a hospital, so the atmosphere of the waiting area is important and this problem has to be addressed by the client, the brief and the architect.

Without denying the beneficial aspects of progress in medicine and treatment methods, and the relevant functionality at the very start of our work on healthcare projects, we were determined in our design not to lose sight of the influence of the environment on patients, medical staff and visitors.

THE HEALING ENVIRONMENT

The concept of a healing environment is rooted in long-standing traditions of complementary medicine and holistic healing. Nature, daylight, fresh air and tranquillity play an important role in the design of healing environments. There is clinical evidence that views of nature, whether it is an enclosed courtyard or an internal garden, are beneficial to people's health. Equally, natural daylight brings a feeling of normality and affects people's mood and performance in a positive way. In our buildings, where possible, daylight through windows or glazed roofs is integrated, as an environmental and low-energy policy, and also for its healing quality.

As part of our general sustainability concerns, we use natural ventilation in hospitals except where it is excluded on medical grounds. The external noise factor, depending on the given site, can be, to some extent, mitigated by the building layout, with a quieter location preferred for wards, with administrative and technical sections located in the

Connolly Hospital – courtyard

Naas General Hospital – Intensive Care Unit

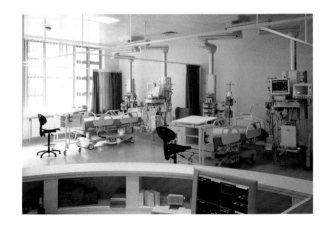

'buffer' zone. Additional elements of the healing environment are in the domain of interior design. Appropriate choices of finishes, colour and texture greatly enhance the internal acoustics and create a desired atmosphere.

Somewhere in this subject area there is a question of the external image of hospital building. It is traditionally associated with a functional technical institution. For a patient it is bad enough to be ill, but to be confronted with an image of a regimented, frightening and inhumane monolith will only exacerbate the situation. When conceiving Naas General Hospital, we decided to steer the design towards the familiar image of a small Irish town. The buildings, with their gable walls, pitched roofs, plaster of various colours, create the very specific character which integrates well into this image. Today, after sixteen years of phased development, Naas General Hospital sits comfortably amid residential estates as a friendly neighbour in its scale and character.

SPACE ORGANISATION

The other aspect of the design philosophy to which we subscribe is a common sense in circulation layout. Connectivity between departments should be short, easy to trace, and pleasant, with intermittent views of landscape, gardens and patios. The importance of circulation clarity from entry to destination is of prime importance. The sick patient, confused and worried relative, or rushing medical staff can be helped immensely by a short and easy-to-follow layout, allied with intelligent signage and informative colour schemes. The circulation routes should also avoid undesirable traffic crossings where contamination may occur. The multi-level 'hospital street' resolves all these issues and is designed on three levels:
• level 1 distributes supplies and removes waste
• level 2 channels visitors to the wards and ambulant patients between various departments
• on level 3, patients are conveyed between departments.

The individual departments connect at right angles to the street, forming landscaped courtyards in-between. Such a flexible layout facilitates phased development, changes in the brief, and, above all, growth in unpredictable stages. A time factor, often influenced by funding, is one of the key issues in hospital planning; good design should recognise this. On the basis of two completely different hospitals, I would like to briefly indicate how our design theories are working in practice.

NAAS GENERAL HOSPITAL *(project architect: Martin Carey)*

Naas General Hospital is located on 3.5ha site, and includes an existing workhouse dating from 1840. In 1986 a Development Control Plan for a new enlarged hospital was prepared. The first phase – the psychiatric department – was completed in 1989, and an updated Development Plan followed in 1998. The main aim of this plan was a harmoniously phased development, during which the old buildings would gradually be replaced by the new, whilst simultaneously maintaining the integrity of the hospital services. Therefore, efficient communication within the hospital

Connolly Hospital – bright interior

Naas General Hospital

organisation was a design priority, as was the creation of a pleasant space for people. The internal 'hospital street' was established on three levels. The site and its surroundings suggested planning the different departments on both sides of the hospital street:

- The lake-side of the hospital complex to the south of the hospital street, with its fine views towards the park, lakes and a southern orientation, was chosen for in-patient departments where patients stay; general and surgical wards, geriatric and psychiatric units, could enjoy these advantages.
- The road-side of the hospital to the north of the hospital street offers short and direct external access, therefore the following departments are located there: accident and emergency, administration with the main entrance, out-patients, day services, physical medicine, and all technical departments.

These basic planning principles created a simple, efficient planning framework, within which fluctuations and change throughout all phases took place without affecting these principles.

CONNOLLY HOSPITAL, BLANCHARDSTOWN *(project architect: Helen Giblin)*

The James Connolly Memorial Hospital was originally built for the treatment of TB in the 1950s. Advances in medicine virtually eliminated TB as a disease, so the hospital turned its attention to current medical and surgical needs, and now serves Blanchardstown and the rapidly growing north-western perimeter of greater Dublin with a catchment area of approximately 250,000 people.

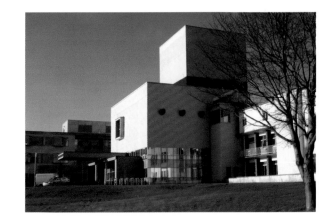

this page and opposite – Connolly Hospital, Blanchardstown

A&D Wejchert & Partners were asked to prepare a Development Control Plan (DCP) incorporating an allocation for all departments and activities, and allowing for future expansion. The design is based on the 'hospital street' concept – a central artery/corridor from which access is obtained to all departments. This 'street' is a multi-layered spine. It provides a general street at ground level leading to departments serving large numbers of the public. The floor above is a 'medical street' leading to more technical areas – surgical day services, operating and ICU. The level above again is a walk-through services corridor serving the entire building.

Mature trees surround the site. The ward block is located at the south side of the building. Angled windows in wards give views towards the Dublin Mountains. The decor is chosen to reinforce the bright airiness – pale timber and a generally light palette with stronger colours in places for emphasis and orientation. A services tower provides a focal point externally beside the atrium. While healthcare projects demand rigorous functionality, they must never be allowed to lose the humane aspect of the design.

As architects know, clinical tests being carried out are starting to prove that good design and a pleasant environment – sunlight, views, calm and quiet – improve healing. Blood pressure is reduced, self-dosing painkiller usage declines, and hospital staff numbers are reduced. Good design helps healing and saves money. It's official!

----

first published in *Architecture Ireland*, °213, January 2006, pp.48-49

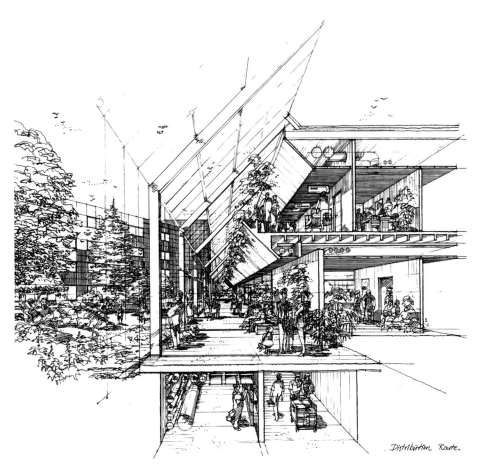

1 – Treatment and diagnostic department
2 – Out-patient department
3 – Wards

4 – Administration and teaching department
5 – Service department
6 – Hospital street

Distribution Route.

Tallaght General Hospital
Competition

This 800-bed-hospital plan offers a simple solution to the complex organisation of many disparate elements and functional demands which a hospital must include. A major internal access route, 'a hospital street', links all the major departments and levels so that they may interrelate and expand. On one side of the hospital street are the wards (3), and on the other the treatment and diagnostic department (1); out-patient department (2) teaching department (4) and service departments (5).

The hospital street is designed on three levels: level 1 distributes supplies and deals with waste removal; level 2 brings visitors to wards and ambulant patients to various departments; and level 3 conveys patients between departments.

address – Tallaght, Dublin 24
design – 1985
area – 62,000m²
note – shortlisted for 2nd stage of competition
hospital planning consultant – Jeff Schmidt

Development Control Plan
Naas General Hospital

Naas General Hospital is located on a site and in buildings originally constructed in 1840 as a workhouse, with various buildings subsequently added. The aim of the Development Control Plan was to indicate a harmoniously phased development during which the old buildings were gradually substituted by the new, while simultaneously maintaining the integrity of the hospital service during all phases of the development. Therefore, efficient communication within the hospital organisation was a design priority, as was the creation of pleasant spaces for people. A hospital street was established on three levels:

level 1 – to distribute supplies and deal with disposal
level 2 – to channel visitors to wards and ambulant patients to various departments
level 3 – to move patients and services between departments.

The general, geriatric and psychiatric wards are located along the quiet lake side of the hospital street. The accident & emergency department, administration and main entrance, out-patients and technical departments are located along the road side, providing easy access for all users of services.

address – Naas, Co Kildare
design – 1986
area – 19,000m²
client – Eastern Health Board
hospital planning consultant – Jeff Schmidt

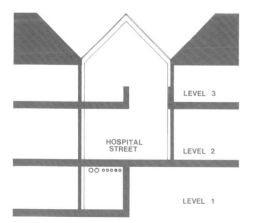

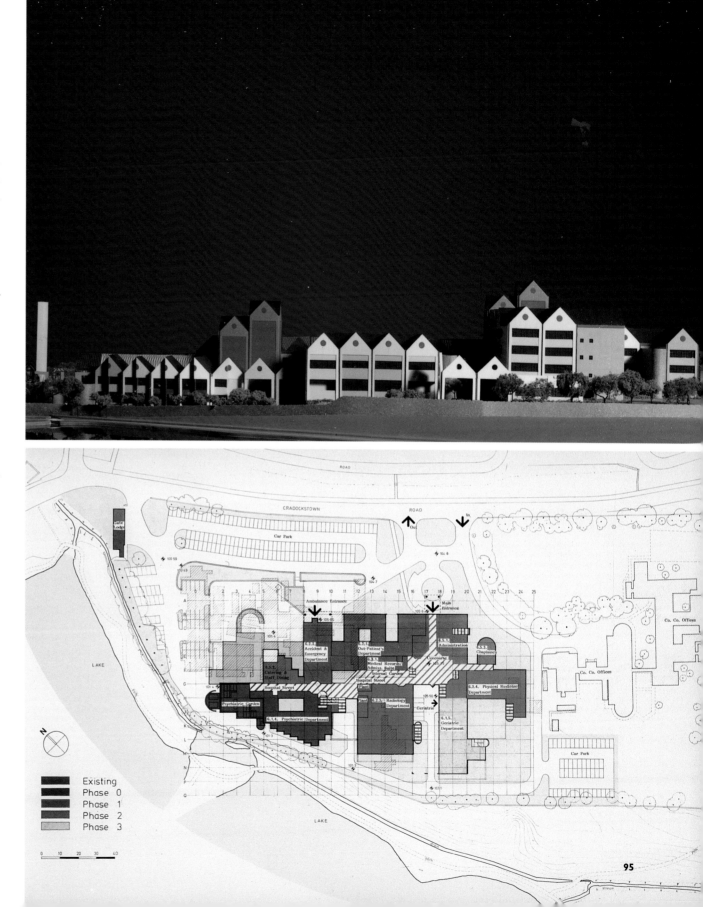

Psychiatric Unit
Naas General Hospital

The main façade of the psychiatric unit of Naas General Hospital faces the south and west, and has fine views towards the ponds in the public park. The unit adjoins the hospital street, of which relevant sections are included in this project.

The psychiatric unit is designed on two levels: the lower ground floor and the upper ground floor. Bedroom accommodation for in-patients (1) is located on the lower ground floor, while day activity areas (2) are on the upper ground level. The garden, closely related to day activities, is located on the higher ground-floor level.

The unit is designed within a planning/structural grid of 7.5m. Elements such as the gable walls, pitched roofs and plaster of various colours create the very specific character of this building which integrates well into the image of a small Irish town.

address – Naas, Co Kildare
design-completion – 1986-1989
area – 2,500m²
client – Eastern Health Board
awards – RIAI Regional Award 1990
hospital planning consultant – Jeff Schmidt

Ground and 1st floor plans – key:

1 – Bedroom accommodation

2 – Treatment/consulting rooms

3 – Education rooms

opposite – View from lakeside

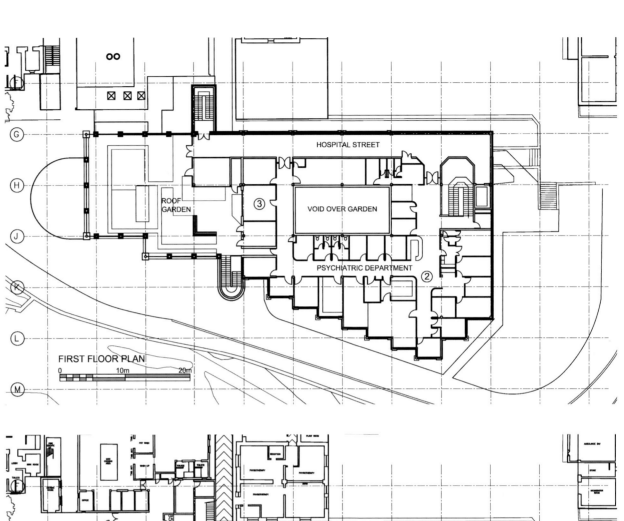

FIRST FLOOR PLAN
0   10m   20m

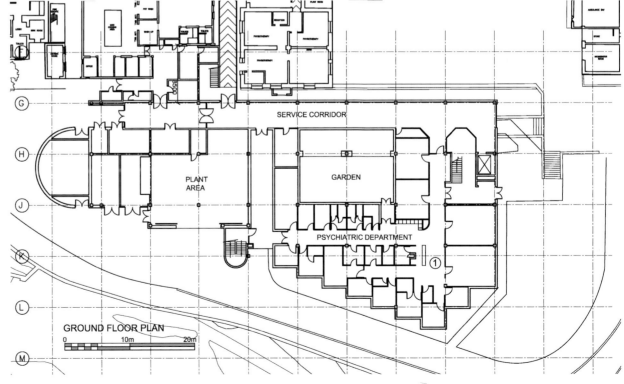

GROUND FLOOR PLAN
0   10m   20m

PSYCHIATRIC UNIT, NAAS

Hospital street

opposite

– Window detail

– Nurses' station

– Dayroom

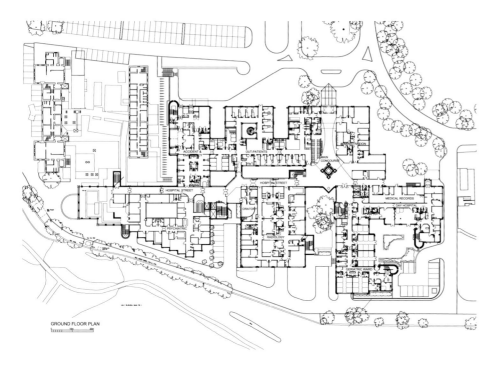

GROUND FLOOR PLAN

Naas General Hospital

address – Naas, Co Kildare
design-completion – 1998-2003
area – 19,000m²
client – Eastern Health Board

―――

above right – Aerial view from lakeside
opposite – View of the wards

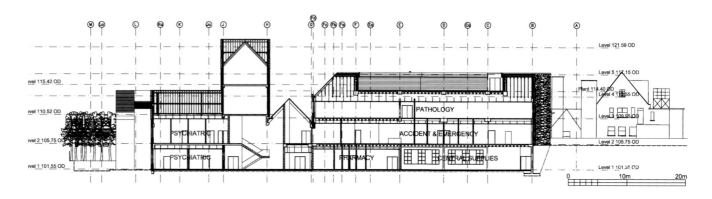

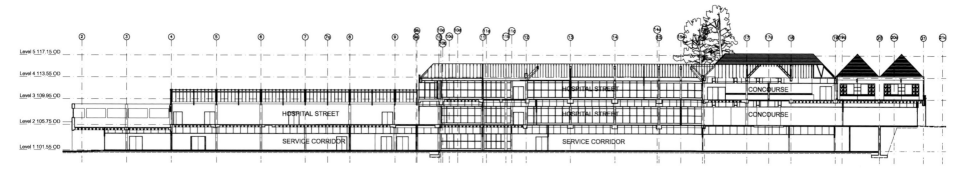

Since the initial construction of the psychiatric department, Naas General Hospital has undergone a number of phases of development in line with the principles of the Development Control Plan, the most significant of which was completed in 2003 and involved creating new in-patient, surgical, administration and rehabilitation facilities arranged around effective and efficient 'hospital street' corridors. A new entrance/concourse was also formed to create a central hub, allowing for connectivity to all hospital functions.

The placement and layout of the building was influenced by the desire to retain the existing mature trees on the site, and in doing so they have enhanced the context of the building. The introduction of a perimeter circulation ring road improves the layout and structure of this relatively compact site.

address – Naas, Co Kildare
design-completion – 1998-2003
area – 19,000m²
client – Eastern Health Board

NAAS GENERAL HOSPITAL

Hospital street

Observation unit

opposite – Concourse

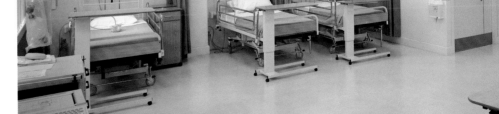

Swords Health Centre

This community health centre is intended as a major element in the integrated community health services for the Swords area. The site faces Swords Castle, and slopes towards the Ward river and the public park in front of the castle. In response to the shape of the site, the building is L-shaped facing the castle and village, and also embraces the view from the village. It acts as a visual shield to industrial buildings behind the site. Waiting areas are situated on the east side of the building to allow the public to look at the river, the open green space, and the castle.

address – Swords, Co Dublin
design-completion – 1996-1998
area – 1,300m²
client – Eastern Health Board

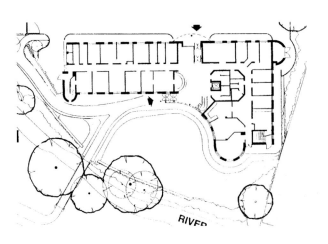

Connolly Hospital

Connolly Hospital, an acute 400-bed hospital, was originally built in the 1950s for the treatment of TB. When advances in medicine virtually eliminated TB as a disease, the hospital turned its attention to current medical and surgical needs.

A Development Control Plan was prepared in 1999, incorporating the existing surgical block and nurses' home into the new development. The new accommodation, finished in 2003, includes an accident & emergency department, operating department, intensive care unit, day services, coronary care unit, psychiatric department and six wards.

The design is based on the 'street' concept of a multi-layered spine from which access is obtained to all departments of the hospital, with a three-storey atrium at the main entrance.

The new hospital is designed to complement the original Scandinavian-type buildings, with extensive fenestration throughout, with solar blinds and sunshades as appropriate, and with views across the surrounding parkland. Angled windows in wards facing east and west give views south towards the Dublin Mountains.

The decor is chosen to reinforce the bright airiness – pale timber and a generally light palette with stronger colours in places for emphasis and orientation. The services tower provides a focal point externally beside the atrium.

address – Blanchardstown, Dublin 15
design-completion – 1998-2003
area – 19,600m² (phase 1)
client – Health Services Executive (HSE)
hospital planning consultant – Danish Health Group

1st floor

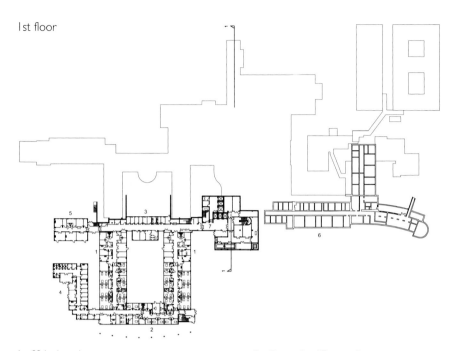

1 – 22-bed wards
2 – High observation ward
3 – Psychiatric department
4 – Psychiatry of Old Age department

5 – Occupational Therapy department
6 – Original hospital building
7 – Hospital street

3rd floor

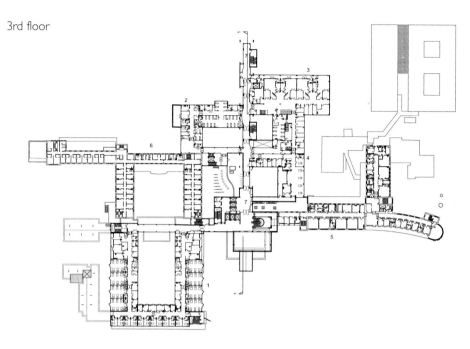

1 – Medical in-patient standard wards
2 – Surgical day department
3 – Operating department
4 – Intensive care unit

5 – Department of Medicine: older people assessment
6 – Original hospital building
7 – Medical street

2nd floor

1 – Dept of Rheumatology / medicine / surgical ward
2 – In-patient non-standard ward
3 – Coronary care unit
4 / 9 – Future / temporary out-patient department
5 – Accident & Emergency

6 – Oratory
7 – Future physical medicine
8 – Dept of Medicine: older people rehabilitation
10 – Original hospital building
11 – Hospital street

4th floor

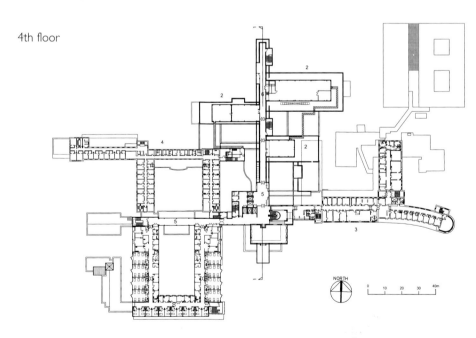

1 – Medical in-patient standard ward
2 – Plant area
3 – Future out-patients dept / Medical day care unit

4 – Original hospital building
5 – Medical street
6 – Services

NORTH

0   10   20   30   40m

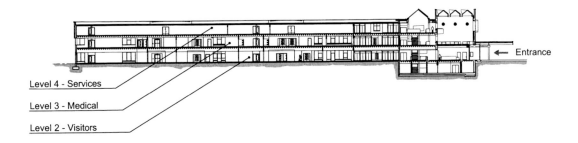

Level 4 - Services
Level 3 - Medical
Level 2 - Visitors

← Entrance

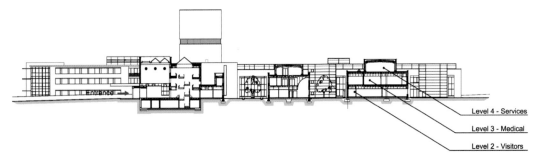

Entrance →

Level 4 - Services
Level 3 - Medical
Level 2 - Visitors

CONNOLLY HOSPITAL

Circulation adjoining concourse
Hospital street

opposite
Hospital street
Concourse

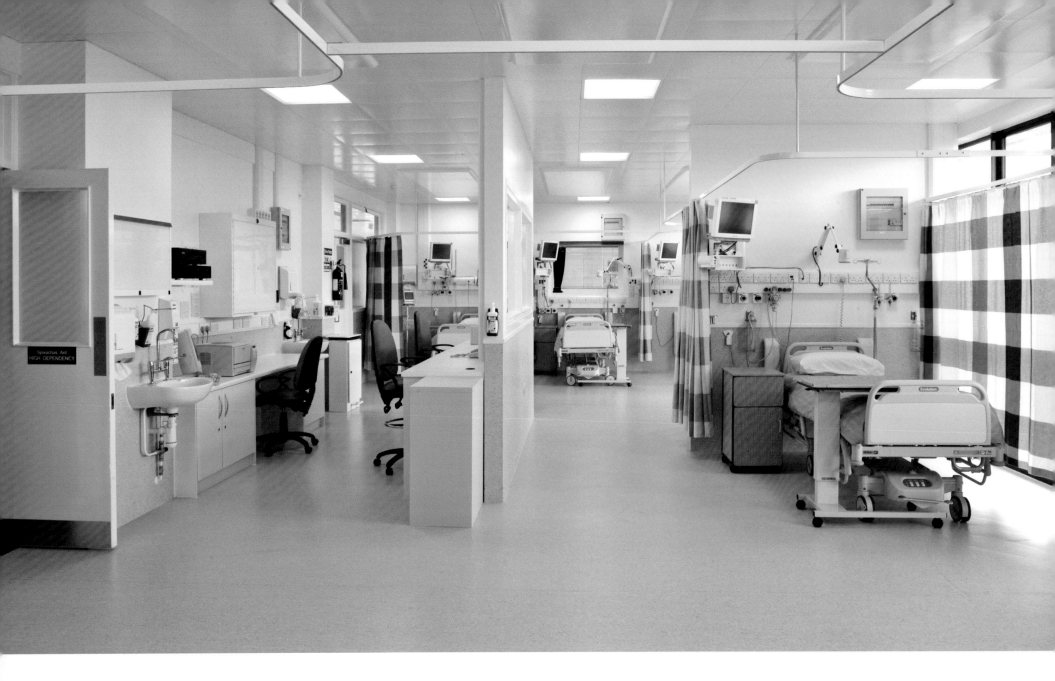

Intensive Care Unit
Drogheda Hospital

This project involved the refurbishment and upgrading of an existing department to accommodate a new intensive care/coronary care unit within the east wing of Our Lady of Lourdes Hospital.

address – Our Lady of Lourdes Hospital, Drogheda, Co Louth
design-completion – 2003-2004
area – 530m²
client – North Eastern Health Board

Accident & Emergency Department
Drogheda Hospital

The proposed new accident & emergency department for Our Lady of Lourdes Hospital in Drogheda is situated to the south of the existing hospital. The unit will consist of approximately 1,250m^2 of new accident & emergency accommodation at ground-floor level, with provision for a new CSSD and ward accommodation overhead on levels one and two respectively.

address – Our Lady of Lourdes Hospital, Drogheda, Co Louth
design-completion – 2007-2008
area – 4,000m^2
client – Our Lady of Lourdes Hospital

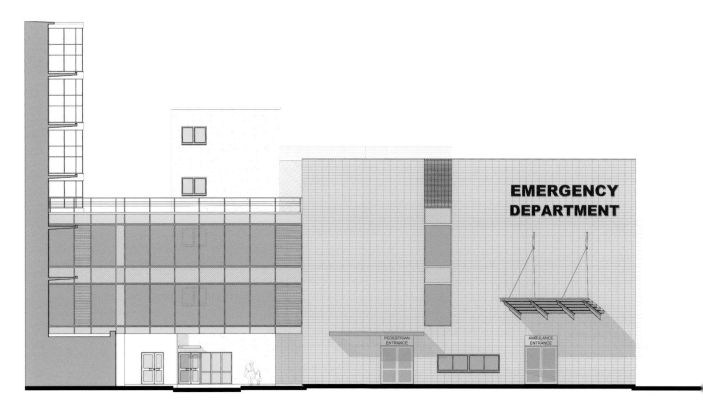

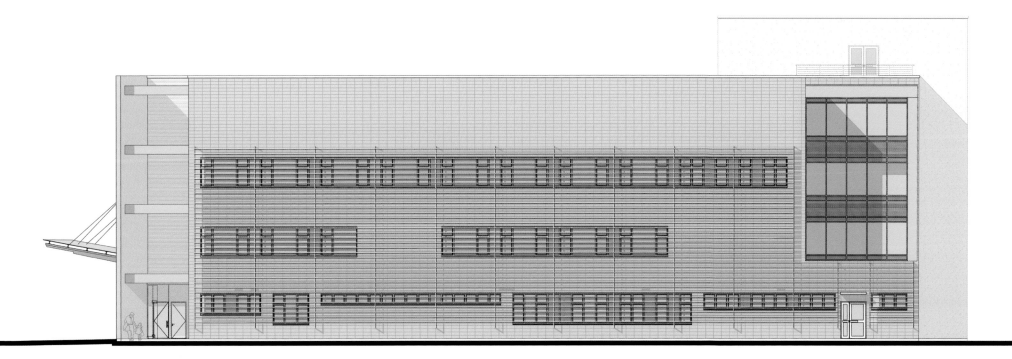

New Healthcare Facilities for Ballymun – Fit-out

This project involved the fit-out of a health centre and offices in the Civic Centre building at Ballymun, spread over three storeys. Part of the new Primary Care Strategy and Ballymun Regeneration, the project utilises vibrant colours, natural light and cost-effective materials to create a welcoming, warm environment which is not forbidding or institutional. The facility is intended to be the focal point for the provision of health and social services in Ballymun and surrounding areas. It offers a unique one-stop-shop diagnostic and treatment facility and minor injuries facility. It provides clinical, social and daycare services and a houses the local area HSE offices.

The integration of the brief into the existing building presented a challenge, as the brief was for a series of easily accessible cellular rooms off circulation areas, whereas the existing building was originally created around a multistorey open-plan atrium design. A priority of the design was to resolve the challenges of easy orientation and circulation for the public to a variety of uses within the existing shell of the building.

Natural materials like timber, glass and planting were used to create a contemporary and forward-looking environment. Predominant theme colours, including terracotta, mint-green and aquamarine, are used throughout to provide a unifying colour on each floor so that users can easily identify what floor they are on. Reception areas and focal points are easily identifiable, with graphic symbols and patterns used to define circulation routes and waiting areas. The resulting design is arranged around a series of welcoming, varied and colourful medical 'streets' on each floor level. All visitors to the health centre are met at various reception counters with adjoining waiting areas. All levels include a number of general public day services (e.g. medical clinics) and specialist services (e.g. dental, physiotherapy and psychiatry).

address – Ballymun, Dublin 11
design-completion – 2001-2006
area – 6,050m²
client – HSE

Irishtown Health Centre

This building is a two-storey replacement for the existing Irishtown health centre. The tight site is surrounded by high residential buildings, so the building is designed around a central double-height void. This allows daylight into the central circulation and waiting areas.

The design of the building and the services are very closely integrated to allow low-energy passive control of heating and air-circulation in a sophisticated and subtle way. The central rooflight acts as a venturi. Heat recovery is achieved by a thermal wheel. All air is fresh, appropriate for a medical building. The design is modern but scaled to match the adjoining buildings.

address – Dublin 4
design-completion – 2006-2008
area – 860m²
client – Health Services Executive (HSE)

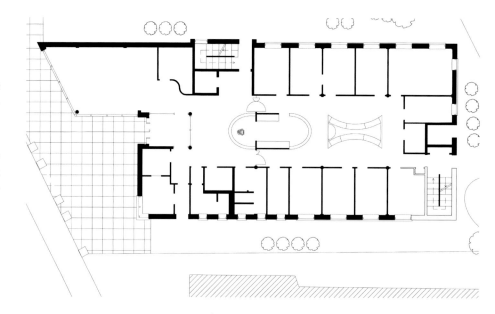

3 – A Place to Shop

Fogal, Fashion Shop
Dublin 2 (1987)

Blanchardstown Centre
Dublin 15 (1996)

page 122

Retail Park, Phase 1
Blanchardstown Centre, Dublin 15 (1998)

Red Mall, Blanchardstown Centre
Dublin 15 (2004)

'Julien', Dundrum Town Centre
Dublin 16 (2005)

Redevelopment of Ilac Centre
Dublin 1 (2002)

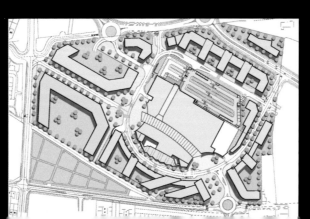

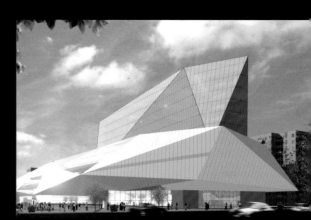

3 – A Place to Shop

In the design of shopping centres we pay particular attention to natural light. In the Blanchardstown Centre a careful balance was achieved between daylight, solar-gain and heat loss, so that the enjoyment of bright daylight would not have to be compromised by the heavy cost of air-conditioning. The pleasant dispersed quality of light is further enhanced by predominantly white and reflective high-quality finishing materials. Sunshine penetrates the glazed roof, and the inclusion of trees gives those sitting outside restaurants and cafeterias the impression of an open-air space. This ambience, combined with generous wide malls, creates a relaxed, stress-free place, encouraging people to return regularly.

Mall study

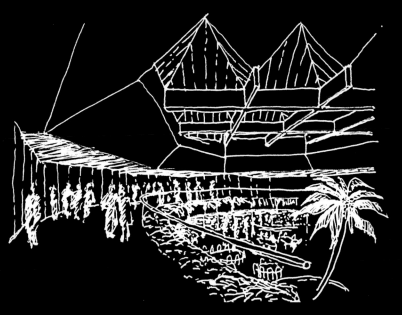

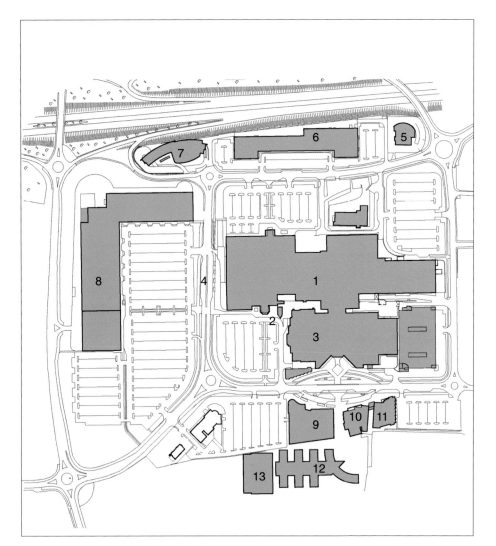

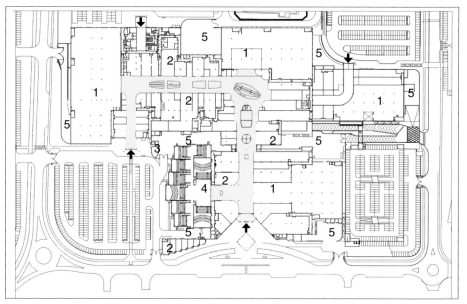

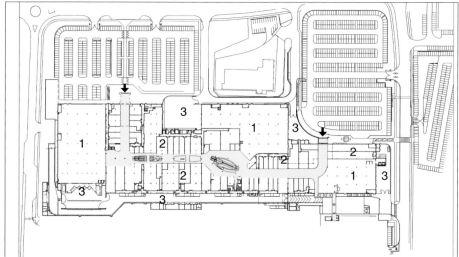

Town centre plan

Upper-level plan

Lower-level plan

Section

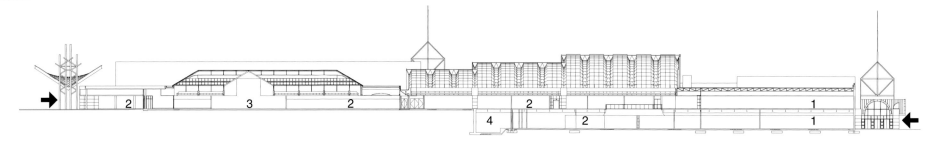

Blanchardstown Centre

Blanchardstown Town Centre in west Dublin consists of the core area surrounded by land designated for ancillary uses, including a park, regional technology college, offices, services facilities, hotel and civic buildings. The Town Centre zone extends over 40 hectares (100 acres). The core area comprises 19.6 hectares (48 acres). The Blanchardstown Centre is a two-storey shopping mall which includes 120 shops, restaurants and a nine-screen multiplex cinema.

In designing the Centre, advantage was taken of the fall across the site. As a result, the lower-level ground floor meets with the higher-level ground floor along a two-storey mall. This arrangement allows for direct and easy access from all the car parks to respective floors. This configuration also hides from public view the main delivery road, and respective delivery yards, under the building.

The complex consists of two easily accessible 'ground floors', which spread in low horizontal planes. The steel-frame structure is clad in clay brick. The friendly, inviting image of the centre is further enhanced by the radiant cream and buff-coloured brick, with some dark-blue engineering brick nearer the pavement. The design of the walls could be compared to a tartan grid, a definite pattern within which dynamic changes in the position of new windows, doors and gates can be accommodated without detracting from the overall effect.

Internally, the space is organised along a two-storey mall,

which joins a central area. Anchor tenants are located at either end of the linear mall, with the large central space featuring a 32m barrel vault. This will be easily identified from the outside as its design is based on graceful semi-circular arches. Units around the central area will mainly consist of restaurants and cafeterias. They relate well to the cinema and library/arts centre in an adjoining location, and together create a vibrant environment for social and cultural activities during evening hours.

A fresh, crisp, bright interior is created by an extensive use of natural light and ventilation, and the selection of internal finishes, including light-reflecting mirrors, ceramic tile flooring, stone cladding and white plaster ceilings and walls. The four

main entrances are highlighted by large pavilion structures with white steel super-structures incorporating coloured sails. Planting internally and externally is abundant.

address – Blanchardstown, Dublin 15
design-completion – 1985-1996
area – 61,000m²
client – Green Property plc

———

BLANCHARDSTOWN CENTRE

Detail of truss, solar protection and glazing
Shops in the central area
opposite – Central area at night

RED MALL, BLANCHARDSTOWN

Mall

opposite – Entrance

Red Mall
Blanchardstown Centre

This extension to a shopping mall at the Blanchardstown Centre consists of twelve new shop units over two levels, and a major anchor tenant over three levels. The new mall links with the existing shopping malls.

This new entrance is heralded by an external sweeping 14m-high curved red wall, and endorsed with a similar internal curved wall, designed to reflect natural light deep into the building, while separating other uses at higher levels. It also also screens the service yard. A monopitch roof structure opens out at the 'elbow' of the mall to introduce extra light into the space.

Externally, the building presents itself as a series of simple geometric forms. Dark-coloured brickwork forms the base of the building, carrying modular references to the existing centre. This base is topped by modular metal panels incorporating signage.

address – Blanchardstown, Dublin 15
design-completion – 2002-2004
area – 12,000m²
client – Green Property plc

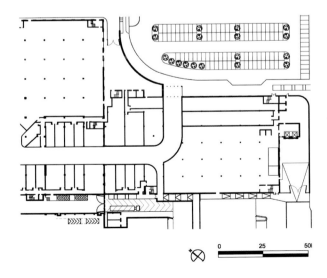

0   25   50l

'Julien'
Dundrum Town Centre

Our brief was to take a small, high-quality boutique and create a contemporary, minimalist image within a reasonable budget on a tight programme – all of which were achieved. The shell provided by the client was an odd shape by virtue of its location, and had a very shallow floor-to-ceiling height. Our objective therefore was to create an illusion of space and light.

address – Dundrum, Dublin 16
design-completion – 2005
area – 180m²
client – Julien Design Ltd

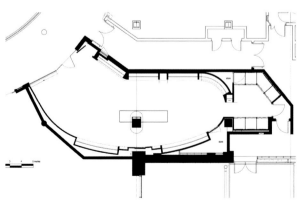

Redevelopment of Ilac Centre

Irish Life was planning a radical redevelopment of the Ilac Centre, Dublin city's largest shopping centre. This project was the winning competition entry for the Ilac development.

The entire external envelope of the Centre is being remodelled, with major emphasis being given to all the main entrances. The proposed stainless-steel entrance cylinders should stand out in the streetscape and be instantly recognisable from every direction, giving a new corporate identity to the centre.

address – Henry Street, Dublin 1
design – 1997-2002
area – 40,000m² (+ 230 apartments)
client – Irish Life plc

South King Street Development

A multistorey fashion centre on South King Street will contain a major store and unit shops, with offices and apartments on higher levels. The building façade reaches out to indicate its presence at second- and third-floor levels. The crystal-like form of the South King Street façade is designed to engage the eye at street level from east and west, up and down the street. Above level 3, the crystalline fragmented form steps back, respecting the scale of the adjacent buildings and forming landscaped terraces for restaurants and apartments.

The façade is almost entirely glass and fully transparent so that shoppers are engaged with the street and passers-by attracted by multi-level display and animation. At street level, the glass façade runs parallel to the footpath to retain flexibility for shopfront arrangements. Above level 1, a faceted glass geometry engages views into the building.

Whilst the architecture is uncompromisingly contemporary, careful consideration has been given to preserving existing vistas towards the Mercer Hospital clock tower and an appropriate interface with the adjoining Gaiety Theatre.

address – South King Street, Dublin 2
design-completion – 2002-2008
area – 10,500m²
client – Chartered Land

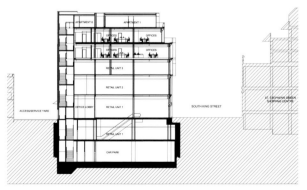

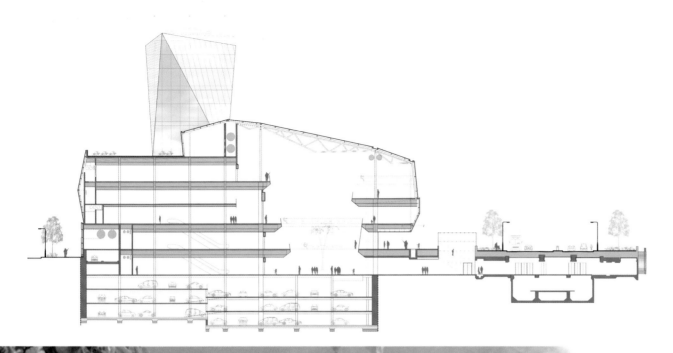

Headland Centre, Warszawa

This mixed-use development is proposed for a dense residential district. It comprises underground parking, retailing on three levels, leisure, entertainment and offices. The lower retail level connects with the metro station. Openness and transparency will characterise the project.

address – Warszawa
design-completion – 2007-2009
area – 100,000m²
client – Headland Property Holding, Polska
associate architects – IMB Asymetria

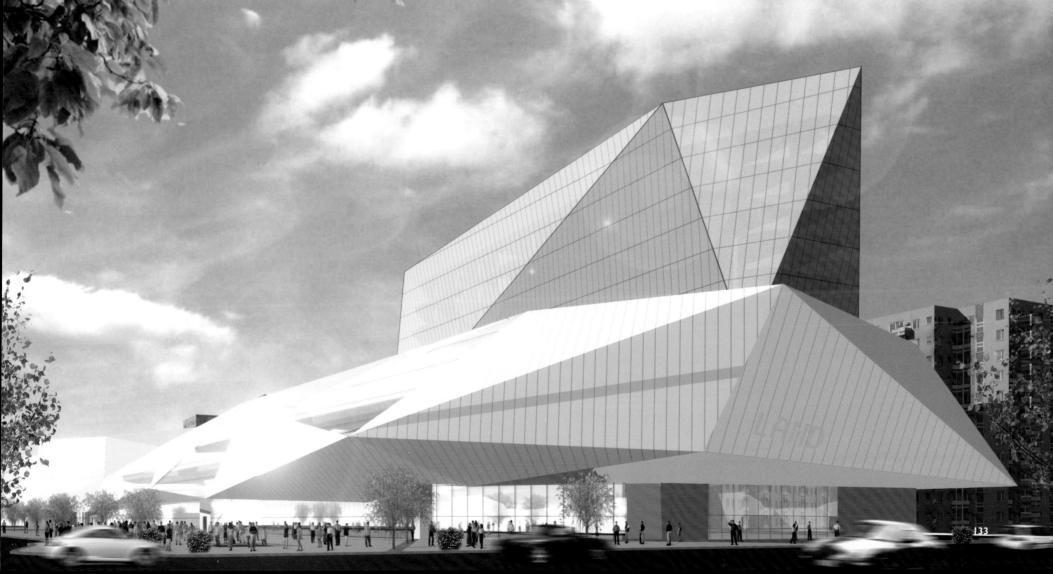

4 – A Place to Work

Bank of Ireland
University College Dublin (1973)

International Organisations, Vienna
– competition (1969)   p;age 140

Small Industrial Units
Clonshaugh, Dublin 17 (1980)

Lombard & Ulster Bank
Lower Mount Street, Dublin 2 (1980)   142

International Business Centre
Castletroy, Limerick (1984)   144

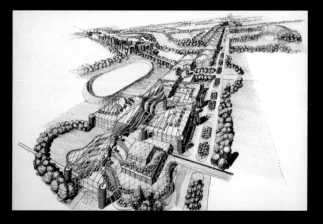

Plassey Technological Park
Limerick (1989)   146

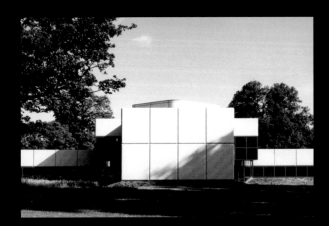

South County Business Park
Co Dublin (1984)   148

Civic Offices, Wood Quay, Dublin 8
– competition (1992)

Custom House Docks, Dublin 1
– competition (1987)

Office Development
65-66 Lower Mount Street, Dublin 2 (1991)   150

Beresford Court
Dublin 1 (1991)   154

Singapore Science Park
Phase 2 (1992)

ITI Corporation Headquarters
Warszawa (1994)

Galway County Council Hall
Galway (1999)   162

Sobanski Palace Complex,
Aleje Ujazdowskie 13, Warszawa (1999)   164

Quinn Direct
Blanchardstown, Dublin 15 (2003)   170

Atrium Office for eBay
Blanchardstown, Dublin 15 (2003)   174

Media Business Centre
ul. Wiertnicza, Warszawa (2002)   176

Irish Cement Offices
Platin, Drogheda, Co Louth (2004)   182

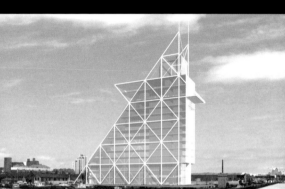

U2 Tower, Britain Quay, Dublin 4 –
Competition (2003)   184

Department of Education and Science
Mullingar, Co Westmeath – Competition (2007)   185

4 – A Place to Work

To the forefront of our design is recognition of the role of the individual within the workplace. For example, in an open-plan office layout we try to promote a working environment of relaxed informality that responds to group and individual needs, and is capable of adapting when needs change. We introduced an atrium with spatial cohesion between it and the open-plan offices. This allows management to overview the entire office at a glance, which could never be achieved in a conventional building.

Media Business Centre, Warszawa (2002)

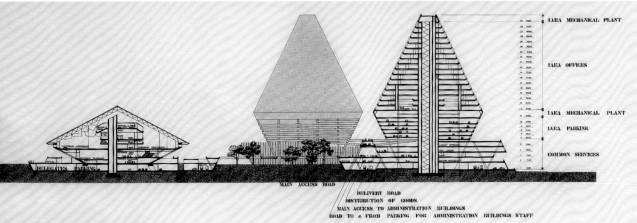

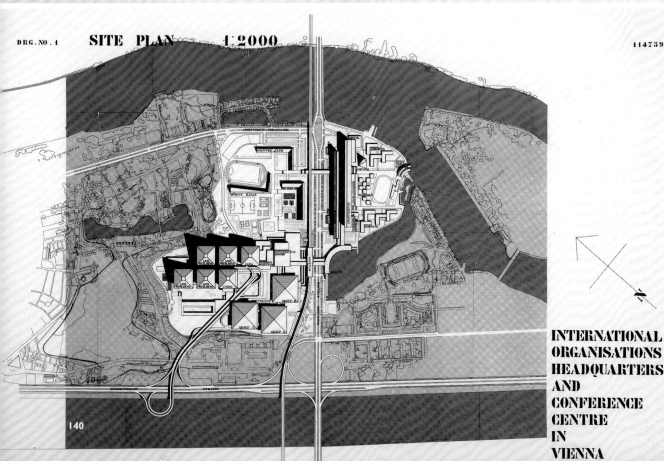

SITE PLAN 1:2000

DRG.NO.4

114759

INTERNATIONAL ORGANISATIONS HEADQUARTERS AND CONFERENCE CENTRE IN VIENNA

International Organisations Centre, Vienna
Competition

The starting point for this development was located in the area of a main public transport junction, where the metro station and bus terminal connect with the express railway. Radiating out from this is the axis of offices, congress halls and residences, in a sequence determined by four constructional stages.

Natural light was allowed to penetrate deep into the office areas of the building through the use of splayed external walls. The part of the building below the offices was reserved for multi-level car-parking. Separate but mutually relating forms of office buildings and congress halls were intended to create a completed environment after each subsequent stage, as well as after the overall completion of this important area of Vienna.

address – Vienna
design – 1969
area – 240,000m² (phase 1)

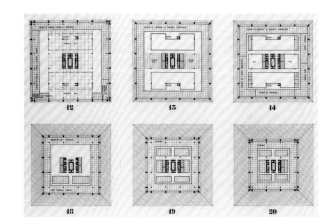

Lombard & Ulster Bank

In making alterations to the entrance (1) and banking hall (2), two main objectives had to be observed – spaciousness and an inviting brightness in the entrance hall, and an intimate and private atmosphere in the banking hall. Mirror-finish stainless-steel panels reflecting the glowing red ceiling were used in the entrance hall. Heavy strongroom-like doors lead into the new banking hall, where attention is drawn towards the centre of the space by a semi-circular counter and the corresponding outline of the red luminescent ceiling.

address – Lower Mount Street, Dublin 2
design-completion – 1980
area – 115m²

opposite – View of entrance foyer with stainless-steel relief by Alexandra Wejchert, 1980

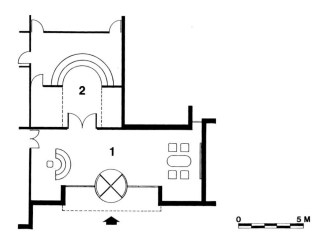

INTERNATIONAL BUSINESS CENTRE, CASTLETROY

left – Site plan / *below* – Development plots / *opposite* – Plan

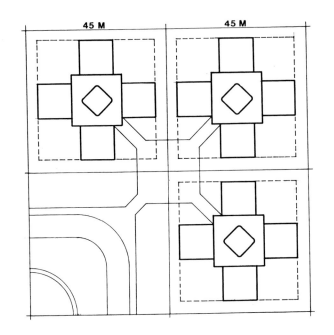

International Business Centre, Castletroy

The objective of the project was to develop the site for high-quality office and research buildings. It is a low-density development with strong emphasis on a relaxed parkland environment. Each cluster of buiildings creates a quadrangle,, with buildings on three sides and a fourth side open to the NIHE complex. The quadrangle will be the focal point of the development and is the subject of special landscaping and an ornamental pond.

There are six plots for separate office buildings, which can be connected if required for a larger use. The buildings, cruciform in plan, are grouped so that each has its main access from the quadrangle. Each building is capable of a 30% extension, which should take place at the rear of the complex. It is envisaged that all the new buildings shall have clay brick to achieve a harmonious relationship with the NIHE, and other new buildings.

The plan consists of four wings and a central octagon with reception, circulation and toilet core. The wings and octagon perimeter contain flexible office space. The plan offers a wide range of accommodation sizes from open-plan concept of 706m² to individual offices of 12m².

address – Castletroy, Limerick
design-completion – 1982-1984
area – 7 ha
client – Industrial Development Authority (IDA)

OFFICE BUILDING, PHASE 1 (1983)

This is a prototype office unit designed specifically for small, high-tech-oriented companies, whose initial space requirements will not exceed 100m². The cruciform plan with central services core is suitable for such subdivisions, giving its users an identity within each wing. The office space is suitable for either open-plan or individual offices, and is capable of partial conversion into a laboratory space.

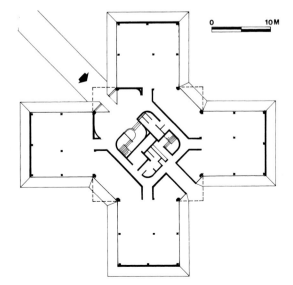

0   10M

145

TO SHANNON AIRPORT/ ENNIS/ GALWAY.

GOLF

Plassey Technological Park

The development of a technological park is a gradually evolving process with aims and objectives being regularly monitored and reviewed. Current developments in this field are leading towards the inclusion of a wider range of uses and community-based activities, such as housing, primary and secondary education, shopping facilities, and community and cultural institutions. This is, therefore, leading to a multi-function concept, with the principal emphasis on its further development as a centre for learning and technological development. In this regard the university is seen as the 'core unit'.

The Civic Centre is conceived as an area located in the focal point of Plassey Technological Park. It bridges the Shannon, creating a strong functional tie between both banks. It is an area which should accommodate all common functions in the park and where people can meet in a 'neutral ground' designated for cultural, social or commercial activities. In order to introduce coherence to such a variety of uses, it is proposed to establish a spatial system which could embrace various functions. It is based on a unit consisting of a glazed roof supported on four circular towers. The towers will contain vertical circulation and all mechanical services. The glazed enclosure will provide a buffer zone between interior and exterior environments. Spaces created by these large atria will accommodate buildings which will, as a result, become more open. Meeting spaces will be created, combating the fragmentation of decentralised organisations in the park.

It is a space of the future with special environmental benefits. The university, research institutes and hi-tech industries will have an opportunity to contribute their inventiveness to the design of energy-saving devices. It should become a development beyond the scale of individual buildings, showing direction towards new social, cultural and technological patterns.

address – Plassey, Limerick
planning – 1982-1989
area – 2,830 ha (7,000 acres)
client – SFADCo

———

right – Civic Centre

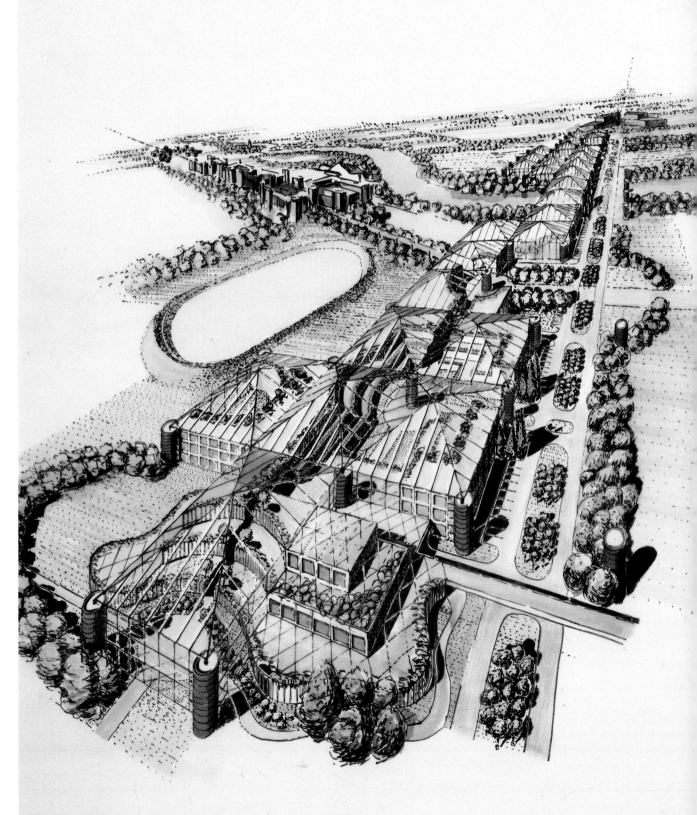

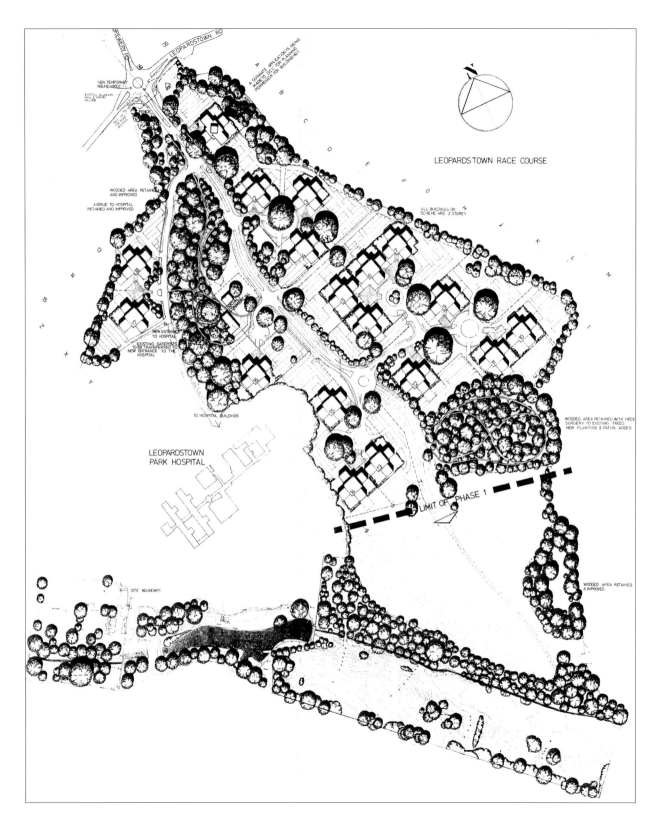

South County Business Park, Leopardstown

Located within six miles of the city centre and approximately two miles from the University College Dublin campus at Belfield, the site was part of Leopardstown Park Hospital, the grounds of which now form the western boundary, with Leopardstown racecourse to the east. The objective is to provide sites for high-quality office and research development buildings in this exceptionally beautiful mature parkland. Only low-density development with a flexible planning layout and small plots for buildings not larger than 2,000m² can meet this objective. The part of the site covered with free-standing single trees was laid out in small plots of between 0.4 and 0.6 hectares. The second site, having trees on the perimeter, will be suitable for larger users, and the third will be retained as an open amenity area. In order to avoid chaotic development, a planning 'macro' grid of 45m x 45m was introduced over the first part of the site. Within the restraints imposed by this grid, and between the trees, buildings are planned in small clusters, thus avoiding unacceptable 'ribbon development'. The main access road branches off into cul-de-sac terminal circular courts, around which two, three or four buildings are clustered.

The building type is aimed towards small organisations. The total area of one building of 2,000m² can be subdivided into offices between 200m² and 300m², or two buildings may be combined into one. The cruciform plan of the building, with a central core and small-scale 'wings', allows for natural lighting and ventilation to all areas. Solid gable walls terminate each wing, allowing the placing of a building close to the road or to parking. In order to maintain a sympathetic relationship between all the buildings, it was decided to limit external exposed finishes to a silver-grey stone-like family of materials, which included stone, concrete and glass-reinforced cement.

address – Leopardstown, Co Dublin
design-completion – 1982-1984
area – 38 ha
client – Industrial Development Authority (IDA)

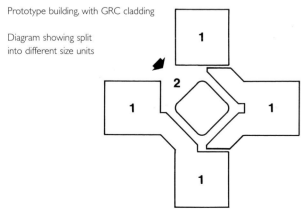

Prototype building, with GRC cladding

Diagram showing split into different size units

OFFICE BUILDING

The prototype building is envisaged as a unit in which young companies in the service or research and development fields will establish themselves on a small scale, and from which they will move to their own building. The brief calls for a naturally ventilated building of between 1,000m² and 1,500m², which could be split into individual tenant units of approximately 100m² each. The plan adopted directly reflects this requirement as each leg of the cross has a floor area of approximately 100m², with tenant units ranging from 100m² to 450m². Each tenant will have a clear identity within the form. All office space is naturally lit and ventilated, and windows overlook a semi-private garden. The form is very efficient from the point of view of ratios between gross and useable floor areas and between gross and external wall areas. Precision-made materials were adopted – white GRC sandwich panels, red aluminium frames and grey reflective glass – reflecting the technological nature of the future users.

address – Leopardstown, Co Dublin
design-completion – 1982-1984
area – 1,350m²
client – Industrial Development Authority (IDA)

Office Development
65-66 Lower Mount Street

The empty site at 65-66 Lower Mount Street presented a considerable challenge. Our clients were anxious to erect a prestigious development which would repair the gap in the street elevation and make a positive contribution to Mount Street and its environs. Extreme care and attention were paid to the urban context of the development, which blends the Georgian character of buildings leading to Merrion Square with the modern character of Grattan House by incorporating some of the essence of each period.

The heavy stone base on the building makes reference to the past, while the delicate glazed curtain wall is more contemporary. It emerges centrally through a brick wall, and steps back at each level. Its projecting bay window is capped by a copper roof, in dialogue with Holles Street Hospital. This centrality is reconfirmed in the side and the rear of the building.

The building recognises the growing importance of creating an identity and individuality in smaller organisations with more flexible work patterns.

address – 65-66 Lower Mount Street, Dublin 2
design-completion – 1988-1991
area – 2,300m²
client – Aranas (Ireland) Ltd
awards – RIAI Regional Award, 1992

Citation – *A powerful mannerist statement, a collision of historic and modernist elements carried out with skill and panache.*
— Irish Architecture 1992 (RIAI, Dublin, 1992), p7

OFFICE DEVELOPMENT, LOWER MOUNT STREET

Reception

Reception counter detail

opposite

Vestibule

Plan and section

152

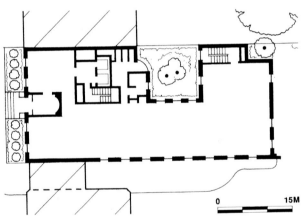

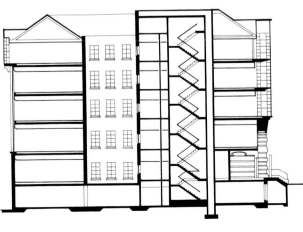

Beresford Court, Dublin

The location and form of Beresford Court reinforces the curved characteristics of Beresford Place around the Custom House, and opens axial views from the Irish Life Centre towards the River Liffey. Its height and scale is related to central Dublin, represented by Lower Abbey Street. Its externally exposed materials and some building elements were resolved to correspond with the surrounding urban landscape. The gross building area of 6,165m² is distributed on six levels over a basement car park, with plantrooms occupying the highest level. Two wings of an average depth of 13.5m form a V-shaped plan, with the main entrance and the lift core at its apex. These wings enclose a central multistorey, top-glazed internal atrium. Light admitted through the glazed roof illuminates the enclosed garden below and adjoining offices.

address – Beresford Place, Dublin 1
design-completion – 1988-1991
area – 6,165m²
client – Irish Life Assurance plc
award – Plan Building of the Year 1992

CRITIQUE
by Arthur Gibney

In the short time since its completion, Beresford Court has made an acknowledged impact on Dublin's urban skyline. Its position, on the awkward junction of Lower Abbey Street and Beresford Place, undoubtedly presented a challenge to its designers. Its siting, fronting on to the newly restored Custom House and a collage of buildings as varied as Liberty Hall, Áras Mhic Diarmuida, the Irish Life Centre and the Financial Services Centre, introduced another level of complications which could hardly be ignored.

The choice of facing material in any building overlooking the Custom House must inevitably start with the consideration of natural stone masonry. James Gandon, in his choice of local granite and imported Portland limestone, followed a traditional Dublin formula which started in Pearce's Parliament House, and continued in the classical ranges of Trinity College and in Thomas Ivory's Bluecoat School. Michael Scott, faced with the problem in the bus station in 1947, opted for part of this formula and used Portland stone. Benjamin Thompson, on the other hand, opted for change, and his recently completed Financial Services Centre used an imported yellow sandstone and a dark local limestone in combination. The result, irrespective of the quality of the building itself, provokes the beholder to ask the inevitable question of why?

The Wejchert partnership's choice of granite for the cladding of Beresford Court has obviously some affinities with the Custom House, but in a complex fashion. The cladding uses a combination of grey and red granite, but in its use of highly polished surfaces it is very different from the austere masonry of Gandon's north façade. Again we are left with the question of why, but

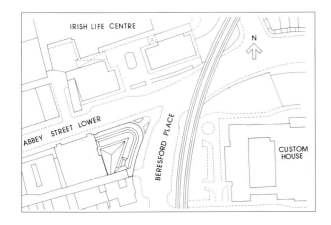

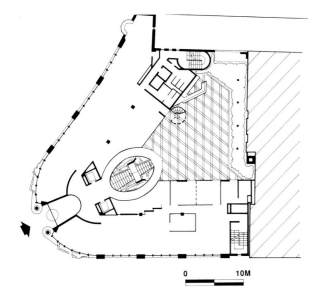

Location
1st floor plan
Section

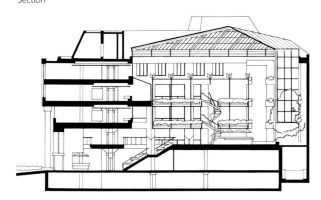

here at least we can grapple with some answers. The significance of the grey granite suggests a relationship with the Custom House and the red granite a response to the adjoining brickwork of the Irish Life Centre and Beresford Place. Is the complex use of different colours and different finishes an attempt to echo the plurality of the building's surroundings?

Whatever about the elusive symbolism of the surface cladding, the resolution of the geometry of the façade has an ordered clarity of intention which is abundantly clear. The major rhythm of the large structural bays alternates with the minor rhythms of granite mullions and window opes, and the interplay of different scales is crisp and sophisticated. The references here are unambiguous. This is essentially the headquarters of a corporate company that is secure in its past traditions, and confident of its future in a building which is unselfconscious of its urban monumentality.

The office accommodation is planned in two conventional width (13m) wings, following the perimeter of the site at Lower Abbey Street and Beresford Place, which come together at the corner entrance in a broad semicircular junction. The difficulties of fitting orthogonal grids into small irregular-shaped city plots is a well recognised problem in urban office architecture, and the decision to develop a strong axis, which bisects the narrow corner junction, provided the designers with a geometric reference which regulates the design. The entrance, framed by two massive granite columns, follows the axis, which develops as the main circulation spine of the plan. The space between the two peripheral office wings and the other site boundary at the Voluntary Health Insurance building is treated as a roof-lit atrium, overlooked both by the offices and by the windows of the neighbouring VHI building.

No aspect of the exterior expression of Beresford Court prepares the visitor for the visual impact of the interior atrium. For a start, the atrium is not positioned on the ground floor but on the first floor and it is approached through a series of carefully designed spatial volumes along the circulation spine, which act as a threshold to its presence. The first of these is a double height entrance vestibule which provides access to a reception area and to the offices on the ground floor. The second is a large elliptical stairwell which introduces oblique views as the stairs are ascended. The arrival at atrium

level and the sudden perception of the volume of the atrium space is immensely dramatic, and as an experience it recalls the spatial climax of a 17th-century Baroque church.

The architectural handling of the atrium lives up to the high expectations of the ascent up the main staircase. The problem of co-ordinating the diverse façades of the office wings and the end wall of the VHI building was solved by the introduction of a secondary elevational grid of white tubular steel sections hung from the structural walls. This continuous framework and the universality of the white Redland cladding unifies the entire interior volume, and provides an ideal background for an extensive interior landscaping programme and Conor Fallen's *Singing Bird* – a 6m-high stainless steel sculpture – positioned precisely where the central axis of the circulation spine terminates in the end wall of the VHI building.

Atria may be exciting places but they can develop complex problems for the design team. Smoke extraction and automatic fire ventilation impose their own disciplines, and awkward collisions of roof glazing and extract vents are commonplace in contemporary shopping centres. Beresford Place avoids all this by arranging the extraction in one horizontal zone at roof level. The only visible sign of the extraction system is a continuous band of aluminium louvres immediately below the roof glazing. Another continuous band of reflecting mirrors – running as a frieze around the atrium at this level – projects the illusion of the roof floating in space without visible supports.

A&D Wejchert consulted with John Worthington of DEGW on the office fit-out, and a full space-planning study established the main organisational patterns of work. The owner-occupiers of Beresford Court (the fund managers of Irish Life plc) opted mainly for an open-plan office layout, combined with a series of conference and formal meeting rooms on the top floor. This promoted a working environment of relaxed informality which responds to group and individual needs, and which can adapt to change as needs arise. The spatial cohesion between the single volume atrium and the open-plan offices allows the entire management style of the owner occupant to be glimpsed at a glance, in a way that could never be achieved in a conventional office building.

Both the interior finishes and the specially designed furniture

of the offices are of a very high standard, and the circulation areas are enlivened by carefully chosen works of art. The red and grey granite used on the exterior carries into selected areas in the interior, and cherry wood is used generally for furniture, panelling and interior screens. The combination of spatial drama in the interior, a relaxed working environment, and high-quality fittings and furniture, adds up to a building package which will repay its owners handsomely for their wisdom in commissioning this imaginative design.

Irish Architect, °88, Jan/Feb 1992 (RIAI, Dublin, 1992)

BERESFORD COURT

Commissioned by Irish Life plc, Beresford Court blends seamlessly into the architectural landscape of central Dublin. The office building has a gross area of 6,165m², distributed on six levels over a basement car park. The architects and interior designers of the building were A&D Wejchert, assisted by space-planning consultant DEGW.

In location and form, Beresford Court reinforces the curved façades of Beresford Place around the Custom House, and opens axial views towards the River Liffey. Its height and scale complement central Dublin, as represented by Abbey Street Lower. The externally exposed materials and building elements were selected to harmonise with the surrounding urban landscape. The two wings of the building, with an average depth of 13.5m, form a V-shaped plan. At the apex are the main entrance and the lift core. The wings embrace a central multi-storey top-glazed internal atrium, which rises not from the first floor, but from the second floor.

The key to this triangular space is the resolution of light, which is admitted through a glazed roof and illuminates the enclosed garden below. The office space is open-plan, with coffee and photocopying stations located centrally near the elevator lobby. The circulation route is clearly identified in the carpet pattern. Meeting rooms are located off the route, with most workstations along the perimeter.

London-based DEGW, represented by John Worthington, were invited by Andrzej and Danuta Wejchert to support

interior planning and fitting out. The aim of the final layout was to provide a strong planning concept with defined zones for support and work areas. Working closely with the Investment Division's consultative team, DEGW assessed future staff needs, drew up workplace standards, and prepared block and layout plans. Research suggested a very different working environment from that of the existing Irish Life Centre, with a balance being struck between personal and shared group spaces. The result of the collaboration is a structure that enhances the productivity of users and contributes positively to the architectural texture of central Dublin.

Office Age, °20 (Itoki, Tokyo, 1993) pp.26-29

BERESFORD COURT

opposite – The stainless-steel sculpture located on the main axis of the building is *Singing Bird* by Conor Fallon

BERESFORD COURT

Board room

opposite

Reception

Exhibition area, with paintings by John Shinnors

Open-plan work space

Galway County Council Headquarters

The building is designed as four three-storey blocks arranged around a landscaped, roof-lit central atrium, which forms the heart of the building and which can accommodate exhibitions. The council chamber is a separate element projecting towards Prospect Hill. Externally, local Galway limestone was used; internally, stonework from the 1802 building was salvaged and used to create one wall of the central atrium. The interior of the building has been designed to create a naturally lit, bright and airy working environment.

address – Prospect Hill, Galway
design-completion – 1993-1999
area – 6,500m²

---

opposite – White concrete sculpture at entrance by Michael Warren

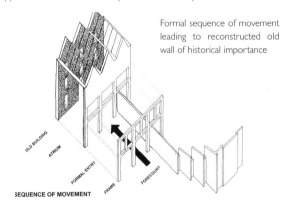

Formal sequence of movement leading to reconstructed old wall of historical importance

SEQUENCE OF MOVEMENT

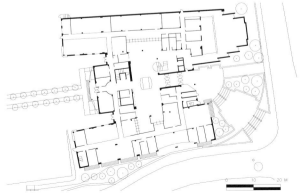

163

Sobanski Palace Complex, Warszawa

The Royal Castle in the heart of Warsaw's Old Town was connected to the king's residence at Wilanow by a 10km-long route. Its name, Royal Way, tells of the splendid processions of the royal entourage in a bygone era.

Sobanski Palace, with its two guard houses, is located on the stretch of the Royal Way named Aleje Ujazdowskie, between the Ministry of Justice and the British embassy, and faces Park Ujazdowski. It was designed by the architect L Marconi, and built in 1876. It has since been altered and adopted to various uses, following the ups and downs of Poland's tumultuous history.

Original guard house (right) with entrance and reception to new office building to the left
opposite – Sobanski Palace (left) and new office building (right), with bronze copy of Donatello's *David* (1430) in the foreground

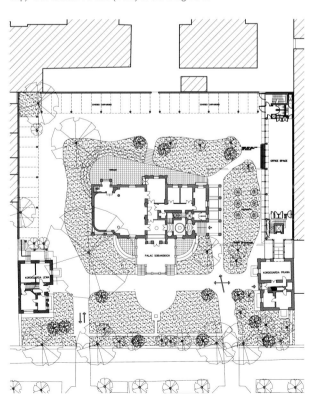

Key decisions – The client wished to house the exclusive Polish Business Roundtable Club within the palace and to erect a new office building against the 16m-tall blank rear wall of the adjoining British embassy. In order to maximise the usable area, the lower ground level of the Palace was lowered in parts to create external patios and to give more light to vaulted cellars, which were converted into drinks rooms. A large modern kitchen, toilets and plantrooms, totally incompatible with the fabric of the old building, were accommodated in an underground basement linking the Palace with the new office building.

The client's wish was to restore the Palace to its former glory, remaining faithful to historical records. Faced with a rich cultural and historical background, the question about the office building had to be answered – namely, should it be dressed in a polite pastiche 'gown' or should it reflect our time? The client and architects were of the same mind. Poland, like France and Japan, tends to cultivate two parallel channels of thought: respect for tradition with a fascination for contemporary culture. This truth is reflected in the Sobanski Complex. The Palace underwent a painstaking historical reconstruction, while the office building speaks of contemporary environmental ideas, realised by using the latest technology and materials.

Environmental elements – The office building provides a contemporary workplace in an open or cellular plan for multi-tenanted or single-occupier user. The design incorporates low-energy, low running-cost solutions in parallel with a comfortable and stimulating internal environment. This direction is the most influential factor shaping future architecture.

The external wall is designed to reduce solar-gain and heat losses, and to direct natural light and air deep into the building while retaining a delicate transparency and lightness next to the Palace. Horizontal shading is provided by aluminium brise-soleil, which extend into the interior and reflect daylight to increase light uniformity. Vertical shading by sand-blasted glass fins cuts off low morning and evening sun. Solar reflective low-emissivity 'K' glass with a 0.4 shading co-efficient reduces solar-gain, but retains partial transparency.

Windows are openable by users at low level, and automatically at high level for night cooling. By exposing the concrete soffit slab to lower temperatures at night, the building is pre-cooled in summer time. Preheated fresh air is ducted under a raised floor to provide floor-based displacement ventilation.

Internally and externally, the materials selected for the office building are a series of neutral silver- and grey-coloured glass, aluminium, plaster and marble. This limited palette provides a simple, sophisticated backdrop to the intricate historic details of the Palace building.

The completed project demonstrates the respect for tradition in the revitalised original Sobanski Palace, and at the same time embraces contemporary architecture and culture in the new office building.

address – Aleje Ujazdowskie 13, Warszawa
design-completion – 1997-1999
area – 2,800m²
client – Wejchert Investments
awards – diploma from Polish Minister of Culture & National Heritage for best modernisation of a historical complex, 2000
associate architects – A Zbiegieni, T Szumielewicz, Warszawa
associate interior designer – Grazyna Prokofi, Bremen

Lowered patio in front of vaulted cellars, with new office building in the background
below – Environmental section
opposite – Garden façade

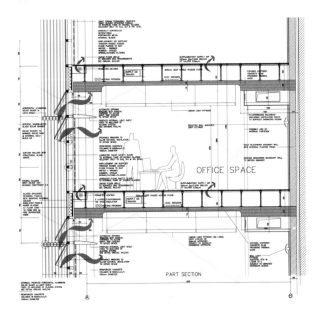

LIFE IN ARCHITECTURE COMPETITION

The Life in Architecture competition is organised by the magazine *Architektura Murator*, in collaboration with the Institute of Polish Architects, the City of Warsaw and the daily newspaper *Gazeta Wyborcza*, under the patronage of the International Union of Architects and Warsaw's Lord Mayor.

The competition was for the best residential and public building completed in 1998-99, for which 136 buildings were submitted. In the category of public buildings, the top award went to A&D Wejchert & Partners for the 'restoration and extension to the Sobanski Palace complex'.

Citation – *Masterly relationships between 20th- and 21st-century high-tech architecture and an ancient palace complex, creating new spatial and artistic values.*

Creative transformation and adaptation of historical palatial residence into new business/commercial functions.

Great architectural culture expressed in appropriate architects' decisions, ranging from the overall spatial/functional idea to the choice of interior design details.

SOBANSKI PALACE COMPLEX

Detail of aluminium brise-soleil and fritted glass fins

opposite – Interior detail

Quinn Direct, Blanchardstown

This office development resulted from a number of factors, including the opportunity to design and construct a pre-let building on the basis of meeting the proposed occupier's specific requirements. These included a site with proximity to the primary road network, good visibility and a high profile, all of which could be accommodated within a high standard of design, compatible with the requirements of a town-centre location and the amenities of adjoining areas. The building was subsequently acquired by Quinn Direct.

The Blanchardstown context – Completed in 1996, the Blanchardstown Centre is approached from both Dublin and Navan via the N3, which is sunken alongside the Centre. The existing buildings are predominantly single and two storey, and therefore largely hidden from this main access road. Located at the north-east corner of the Centre, adjoining the N3, Site K (as the site was originally known), offered a unique opportunity to create a quality landmark building to act as a flagship in announcing the Centre's presence.

Comprising a large number of mainly retail units, the Blanchardstown Centre also accommodates services units, a

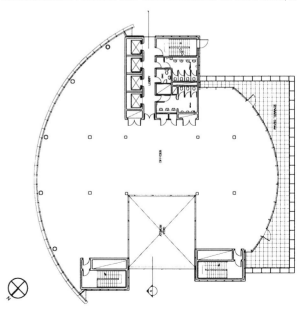

medical and amenities block, an oratory, leisure and recreation facilities. Draoicht, a major arts and civic centre with theatre and library facilities, opened in 2000. The introduction of offices widened the variety of uses within the town centre, thus fulfilling one of the principal objectives of the County Development Plan.

The building – The building's form was generated by an end-user requirement for 8,000m^2 of usable office space. This is distributed in a U-shaped floor-plan configuration around an atrium. The relationship of the atrium (treated as a buffer zone) with the surrounding office area, the building's orientation and the choice of materials used places the design of this building firmly amongst those searching for sustainable, low-energy solutions. This approach met with the client's wish to rely on natural ventilation and natural light.

The entrance to the building is through the atrium, which rises through the entire ten floors. Offices are naturally ventilated, and raised access floors and ceiling voids create a network for power, voice and data cabling distribution.

Externally, the offices are treated in curtain walling, with a curved wall facing the N3, reflecting the dynamism of that thoroughfare and of the adjoining bridge. Cores are expressed externally, and clad in a selected monochromatic insulated metal-panelling system.

Vistas of the building are dramatic, as are the views from the building; particularly from the penthouse and upper floors where there are views east towards the Dublin Mountains and north towards the airport. These offices are another major step in the urbanisation of Blanchardstown, an elegant addition to Fingal's developing economy.

address – Blanchardstown, Dublin 15
design-completion – 1998-2003
area – 8,000m^2
client – Green Property Ltd
awards – Opus Building of the Year Award (commended)

QUINN DIRECT

Rooftop boardroom
Main entrance façade

opposite – View from under the motorway bridge

ATRIUM OFFICE

Atrium with structurally glazed wall

Ground-floor plan

opposite – View from motorway

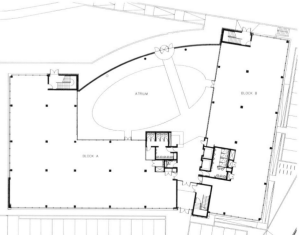

Atrium Office for eBay, Blanchardstown

The Atrium is a shell-and-core office building suitable for fit-out. It comprises two five-storey blocks surrounding a glazed atrium on three sides. Naturally ventilated through the windows on the external wall, the offices enjoy the amenity of the atrium, which acts, at once, as a central focus for the occupier, a place to relax, a magnificent entrance experience and as a buffer against the noisy motorway.

The two blocks are sized to generate optimum subdivisibility into either twelve separate lettings or a single one. They are extremely simple, standard 13m-wide blocks with a 3.6m floor-to-floor height. It is the manner of their arrangement around the north-facing atrium that provides spatial interest and the opportunity to create a unique imagery through the structure.

Clad externally in aluminium and curtain walling, the offices are clad in oak sheeting where they face onto the atrium space. This creates warmth and a good acoustic quality in a space that is otherwise formed in glass, steel and ceramic tile.

Functionally, the atrium space offers a variety of uses which are adaptable to the letting programme. Landscaped with trees and shrubs in movable tubs, the space lends itself to being used as a reception hall, a location for customer interface kiosks, or simply a social area with cafeteria facilities. An elliptical suspended ceiling of white plaster, whose shape and form define the foreground, masks the random plan geometry and basic structure of the atrium roof. Linear rooflight lanterns admit natural light through the roof adjacent to the offices. Air is taken in through the openable windows at the perimeter, heated by the occupiers, and entrained through the atrium's internal perimeter wall to be entrained up and out through its roof.

address – Blanchardstown, Dublin 15
design-completion – 2001-2003
area – 6,000m²
client – Green Property Ltd

Media Business Centre, Warszawa

This building was commissioned by ITI Corporation in 1995. The brief was developed over several years, and was finally defined as a headquarters for television, film, advertising and internet companies using the most up-to-date information technologies. The site is south of the Warsaw city centre, at the major road intersection of ul. Wiertnicza and ul. Augustowka. The site boundary adjoins a green belt area at the rear. The previous ITI headquarters building (1990-1994) and TVN studios are located beside the site.

The massing of the building has been designed to address urban concerns. The building was to conform to the four-storey height along ul. Wiertnicza, but could rise towards the green belt end. It was also to relate to a diagonal axis towards the road intersection, as the previous ITI headquarter building did. As a result, the building form is stepped. It consists of three vocabularies — translucent glazed office floors, vertical stone service towers, and a tilted arch of the glazed roof, embracing two atria.

Internal Planning

Internally, the space is formed around two atria, one at ground level and the other at first-floor level, in a plan resembling the figure 8. The central internal block between the two atria accommodates glass stairs connecting two atria. As the project brief stipulated that there must be natural light and natural ventilation in all offices, the two atria are glazed and

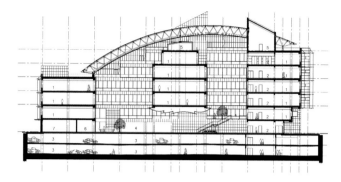

ventilated using fully glazed roofs arching over the building, with ventilation panels.

The first two levels are underground and contain parking for 360 cars, connected by lifts to the offices above. The ground-floor area around the atrium contains restaurants, cafeterias, bars, shops and a bank, to serve a population of approx 1,500 people. A conference suite, a 'business academy' and a building management centre are also on this level.

A large, 24-hour television news broadcasting studio is locat-

MEDIA BUSINESS CENTRE

Balcony to management suite

News broadcasting studio

opposite – Atrium at ground floor, with news studio at 1st floor level

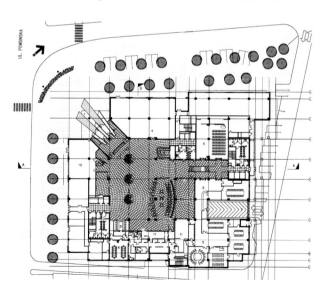

ed at first-floor level, acting as a focal point for the development. The client's intention was to create a studio where the broadcaster could see the public flowing through the atria and visitors could see the studio lights and cameras from the atrium.

Structural materials

A continuous raft foundation with a concrete diaphragm wall was chosen as the foundation system for the development, surmounted by a reinforced-concrete superstructure frame and a steel roof. Restraint has been exercised by limiting the building envelope to stone, glass and aluminium. The same materials follow through to the interior, with the notable addition of limed oak.

The idea of transmission waves became a key motif of the interior design in public spaces. The geometry of curved waves is used in floor and ceiling patterns, seats, counters, walls, all radiating from one point – the TV studio. The media character of the centre is emphasised by the main entrance, which is formed by huge ITI letters pulsating to the rhythm of changing colours.

address – ul. Wiertnicza, Warszawa
design-completion – 1995-2002
area – 32,000m^2
client – ITI Corporation Group
awards – Intelligent Building of the Year Award, Warszawa, 2003
    – Polish Ministry of Infrastructure, Building of the Year 2002 (2nd place)
associate architects – APA Markowski & Partners, Warszawa
associate interior designers – Event Communications, London

MEDIA BUSINESS CENTRE

Stairs connecting ground floor to 1st floor atrium

opposite – Main entrance

Irish Cement Offices, Drogheda

The site for this new headquarters office building faces the main entrance to the factory complex, and therefore demanded a building that would project an appropriate image for Ireland's major cement producer.

The new office accommodates a staff of forty, along with back-up and ancillary spaces. The building is formed with curved concrete walls and freestanding columns, on which the company name is displayed. The device of using the walls, which partially disappear into the earth berms, acts as an organiser of the external space while partially screening the building and directing views towards the silos – the most dominant elements on the site.

The curved, fairfaced, board-marked concrete epitomises the unique plastic quality of in-situ concrete. These curved walls and the round concrete drum containing the boardroom visually integrate the administration offices and the silos of the cement production plant into a symbolic whole.

address – Platin, Drogheda, Co Louth
design-completion – 2001-2004
area – 850m²
client – Irish Cement
awards – Irish Concrete Society Award, 2004

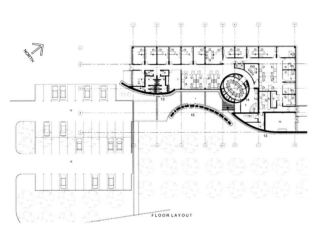

FLOOR LAYOUT

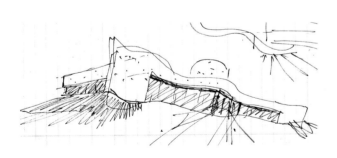

U2 Tower – Competition

There are dramatic distant views and water reflections of the Britain Quay site from at least two principal directions. To achieve a powerful, memorable image in such a location, a simple geometric form is proposed. A triangular building – reinforced by triangulation of the exposed structure – gives a sense of stability and strength. It also acts as a vertical pointer, while evoking memories of docklands, cranes, warehouses and ships. Against this self-confident image, a triple-glazed skin provides a counterbalance of reflectiveness and lightness, changing with the quality of light, the time of day and reflections in water.

Space organisation

Stratification – Level 0 contains a bar, active during the day, becoming a music venue at night. A restaurant located above, on level 1, offers panoramic 360° views towards Dublin and the sea. Ten levels of offices above are capped by the U2 studio on levels 12 and 13. The lowest level (1) is designated for car park, deliveries and storage. The highest level (14) contains the plantroom.

Floor layouts – The vertical core and all enclosed accommodation are located in the central part of the floor plates so that the entire perimeter can enjoy views. Terraces at levels 12 and 13 are provided for the exclusive use of U2, as is the roof garden on level 14.

Structural and external finishes – Steel is used along the perimeter, and a concrete core provides horizontal stiffness. The triple-glazed wall provides environmental control, natural ventilation and solar protection.

address – Britain Quay, Dublin 4
design – 2003
area – 12,000m²

Department of Education & Science – Competition

The form and landscaping of the building is derived from the linear, flowing nature of the river parallel to the site. The building form is composed of two main blocks of office space, curved in different directions to offer a softer physical form to the riverside and a more dynamic elevation to the road. A natural stone-clad gable, and similarly clad 'pop-out' conference rooms, will contrast with the curved glass and aluminium curtain wall elevations with their striking vertical brise-soleil.

The entrance to the building is at its heart, where there is a generous full-height staircase with a large, clear-glazed wall facing the external spaces and the linear park and river. This facilitates easy orientation for all who will use the building. From the central space, all communal functions such as meeting rooms, filing, research library, etc, are immediately accessible. All office space is situated in two blocks either north of south of the entrance volume.

The overall landscape design seeks to make the most of the river by opening up the park along the east bank to the road with selected planting, paved paths and public benches. A pool is being built adjacent to the building to reflect light into the central staircase and to act as a feature to the surrounding offices and canteen. It will also have the practical function of acting as a storm-water attenuation reservoir. The external landscaped areas are being treated as an amenity for the users of the building and the public in general.

address – Mullingar, Co Westmeath
design – 2007
area – 9,000m²
clients – Office of Public Works / Sisk & Son
associate architects – Berham Barry Architects

5 – A Place to Live

House for Herbert von Karajan
– Shinkenchiku Competition (1975)   page 190

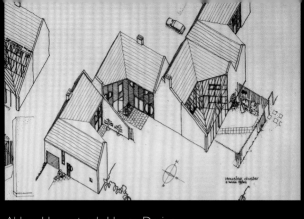

Abbey Homesteads House Design
– competition (1982)

House at Loughrask
Co Clare (1983)   191

Smithfield Village
Dublin 7 (1987)   192

Kotronas Project
Greece (1987)

Residence for Ambassador of Japan
Foxrock, Co Dublin (1998)   198

Heather Cottage
Howth, Co Dublin (2004)   208

House in Adare
Co Limerick (2007)

5 – A Place to Live

Before moving into the design process, we carefully analyse the brief and the lifestyle of our clients, and any special requirements they may have. The emphasis varies from client to client, for example, on the relationship between day and night zones; between formal and casual spaces – all the components that make each house unique. The greatest consideration, however, is given to location, which can render a house design even more unique.

In the case of Ardcarraig House, Galway, the luscious garden was of paramount importance and the house was designed to float above it, catching the views of Lough Corrib in the distance below. Heather Cottage in Howth merges with the traditional stone walls so characteristic of the local landscape, and the profile of the house is kept low, in an almost cave-like manner, so as not to intrude on the spectacular barren landscape on the eastern shores of Howth.

House for Herbert von Karajan – Shinkenchiku Competition (1975)

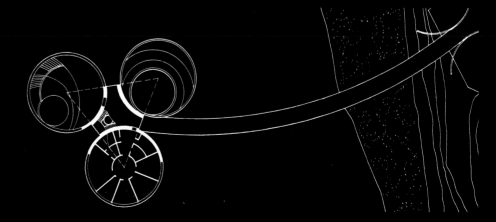

House for
Herbert von Karajan
Shinkenchiku Competition

Located on the Mediterranean coast, the design of this house was developed to give expression to the character and attitudes of its owner.

address – Côte d'Azur, France
design – 1975

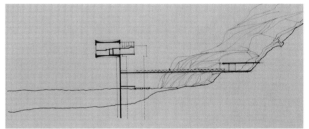

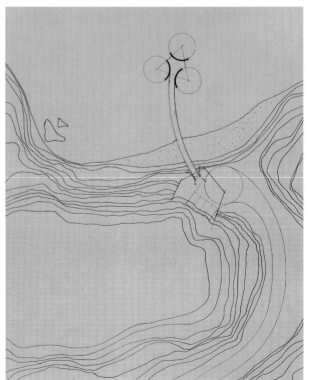

House at Loughrask, Co Clare

The site, on a slightly elevated hill some 300m from Galway Bay, is on the edge of the Burren, an area famous for its limestone rock formations.

The house has an L-shaped plan. A large bay window terminates the diagonal axis originating at the entrance. This bay window was inspired by a similar element (although constructed in stone) in the O'Brien Castle at Leamaneh, originating from AD1480.

address – Loughrask, Co Clare
design-completion – 1979-1983
area – 170m²
client – private

MAISON D'UNE CELIBATAIRE, LOUGHRASK, IRLANDE

The detail of this oriel window made me include it here. This element gives this otherwise simple façade all its poetry. This is the connection between the comfortable man inside and the wild countryside.

— Jean-Pierre Dumont

from *Façades de Maisons Individuelles* (Editions Detta, Brussels, 1985)

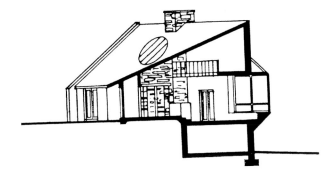

Smithfield Village

Smithfield Village is a mixed development facing onto Smithfield, a large cobbled square in Dublin's north inner city. Smithfield, longer than Rome's Piazza Navona, is a medieval market square and once a busy commercial part of the city. The site was part of a large complex owned by the John Jameson & Sons whiskey distillery (later Irish Distillers). The distillery moved out in the 1970s and the site became derelict, with a maze of stone and brick buildings separated by cobbled lanes and open spaces, all in a ruinous condition.

The brief was for a mixed development of residential, commercial and cultural uses. It was quickly decided to split the uses horizontally – residential above to give views and privacy, and non-residential at street level. On the upper level there are 224 apartments, with a mixture of one, two and three bedrooms, with access to roof gardens. Car-parking is located at basement level, while shops, a sculpture gallery, the Jameson Whiskey Museum, restaurants and a leisure centre are all accessed from street level. A 77-bed hotel, with an adjoining traditional Irish music centre, faces onto Smithfield. The listed 1895 chimney is retained and an observation platform built on top, accessed by a panoramic lift, to allow the public a bird's-eye view of Dublin.

The development is open to the public to give access to the shops and restaurants. Duck Lane, crossing the site from east to west, is reopened and thus provides a pedestrian route from

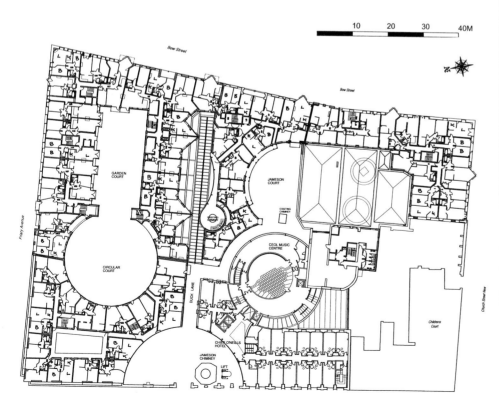

O'Connell Street to Collins Barracks. The aim was to produce a mix of uses in a viable way to create a village atmosphere.

Existing architectural elements worthy of preservation were retained, with new development built in and around them. The circular form of the vats and stills used in whiskey-distilling were found again and again on the site, and this influence is visible in the village layout. There is a deliberate play made between modern construction and the existing elements – for example, the articulated silver cladding versus the massive redbrick and grey limestone walls.

The formidable existing brick wall along Smithfield and the square itself dictated the scale of the western façade. The brick wall was extended with a grand semi-circular access embracing the chimney, in recognition of its large urban scale. Bow Street maintains the character of a narrow, slightly curved street, with a glazed façade stepping back above the stone wall, and with residential towers breaking the stone with crystal-like projections,

Internal courtyards provide a variety of spaces, the scale of which is friendly to inhabitants and passers-by, and which help foster an 'urban village' character in the residential element of the scheme.

address – Smithfield, Dublin 7
design-completion – 1983-1987
area – 30,000m²
client – Heritage Properties Ltd

SMITHFIELD VILLAGE

Residential development along Bow Street

opposite – Residential urban spaces

SMITHFIELD VILLAGE

Extended perforated brick wall of distillery facing Smithfield Square with chimney and observation platform

opposite – Glazed façade to Chief O'Neill Hotel

Residence for Ambassador of Japan

This was a very memorable project, during which we met not only the Japanese client, but also architects, contractors and artisans who were brought from Japan. The main architectural theme was a harmonious relationship between the cultural expressions of two countries, Japan and Ireland.

address – Foxrock, Co Dublin
design-completion – 1995-1998
area – 1,400 m² approx
client – Department of Foreign Affairs, Tokyo
in collaboration with Konichi Nagamatsu Architect, Japan

Addition to Residence at Monkstown

A new two-storey glazed space connects the kitchen at first-floor level with the ground-floor family room and the garden.

address – Monkstown, Co Dublin
design-completion – 1997-1998
area – 65m^2

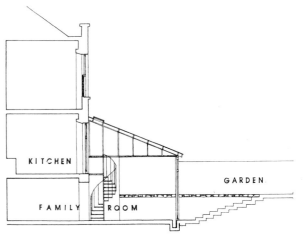

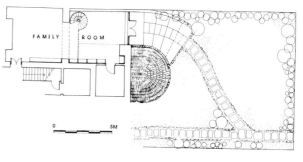

House at Ardcarraig, Co Galway

The house is located in a well-established private garden of exceptional beauty and international repute. It is sited on a north-facing slope close to its site boundary in order to cause as little intrusion as possible.

The design concept was to locate the house on an elevated site to take advantage of the views to the north over Lough Corrib, while ensuring that southerly light is exploited and brought deep into the house. Visual contact with the garden is achieved by the fully glazed north façade, with an even stronger relationship achieved from an open-air balcony jettisoned over the garden.

Advantage is taken of the slope by entering the house from the north side at the top of the slope. All the living space is

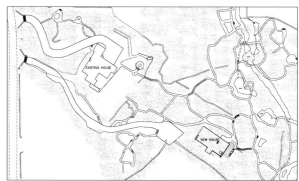

located on a single level, with day-use areas as a single space for efficiency of space and ease of maintenance. The boiler room and ancillary functions are located on the lower level in the base of the building.

All the major rooms, living/dining, kitchen, master bedroom and study/bedroom, are located to take advantage of the spectacular view, while still retaining south light from the split-level roof. A sunroom located at the south-east corner opens to the kitchen, exploiting morning and daytime sun.

A dramatic cantilevered balcony is included at the north-east corner, which is accessible from the kitchen and the sunroom. This balcony, with spectacular views, catches the sun for much of the day. A restrained palette of external materials stone, glass and zinc was used to underline the humble approach of the man-made towards the splendour of nature.

address – Co Galway
design-completion – 2001-2003
area – 148m²

HOUSE AT ARDCARRAIG

Living room with views to the garden and Lough Corrib

opposite – Section, plan and external wall detail

204

Residential Complex with Retail and Offices, Galway

This mixed development close to Galway city centre contains a shop and medical practice at ground level, an office in one wing at first-floor level, apartments above, with parking in the basement. Access to the residences is via a grand flight of steps to a central courtyard.

The 34 apartments are divided into 16 two-bed and 18 three-bed duplex units. Living rooms face outwards to catch the sun and views. The top floor is carried to the underside of the roof to provide a lofty, open-plan living area. Apartment areas are generous, and finishes, which include hardwood floors and fitted kitchens, are carefully selected.

The development is an example of a common urban/suburban feature – a small commercial node in amongst suburban housing, with residential accommodation on the upper levels. The scale and materials are chosen to draw attention to the node without overwhelming the surrounding housing, and to provide a pleasant place to live, with outdoor areas for the residents to enjoy.

address – Fr Griffin Road, Galway
design-completion – 2001-2004
area – 5,003m²
client – Rhatigan Developments Ltd

Façade to Fr Griffin Road
Interior residential courtyard

opposite
Plan on three levels
Urban entrance to residences

206

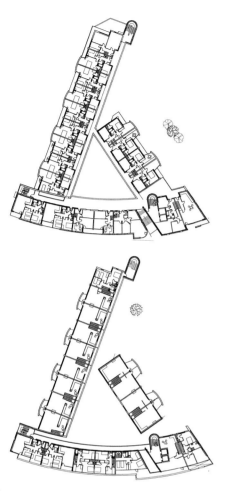

1 – Shop
2 – Medical group practice
3 – Office
4 – Terrace

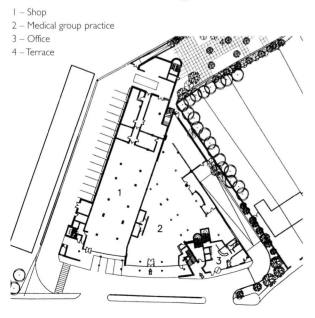

207

Heather Cottage, Howth

This new house is located on a spectacular 350-acre site in an area of great natural beauty, and enjoys breathtaking views of Lambay Island and Ireland's Eye. The form of the house is irregular and organic. Changes of level fragment the scale and help it merge with the contours of the site.

The open plan living areas are orientated towards the dramatic sea views. Windows are recessed or hidden behind rustic stone walls to avoid exposure of reflective glass surfaces, which would be alien to this landscape. Light is also admitted into the interior spaces by subtle roof-lighting in the stairs and circulation areas.

The bedroom wing comprises two levels and has been separated from the living quarters by the entrance hall and stairs. Light and ventilation are brought to the lower bedrooms by a series of external light-wells cut into the hillside.

address – Howth Head, Co Dublin
design-completion – 1999-2004
area – 270m²
client – Treasury Holdings Ltd

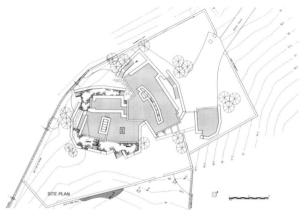

SITE PLAN

HEATHER COTTAGE

South-east elevation

Ground-floor and lower-ground-floor plans

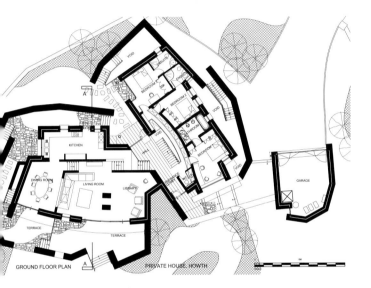

GROUND FLOOR PLAN   PRIVATE HOUSE, HOWTH

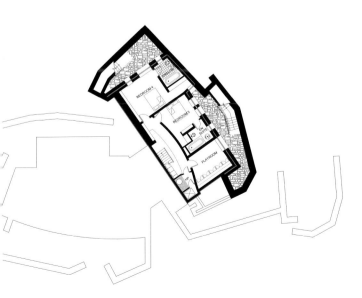

6 – A Place for Leisure

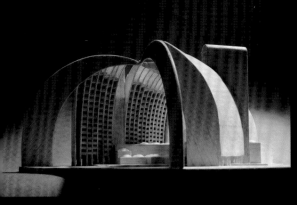

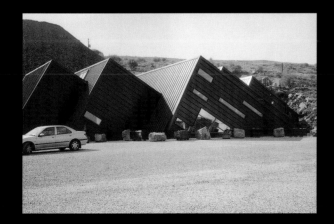

Knock Hotel House
Co Mayo (1999)

Ceol Traditional Irish Music Centre
Smithfield Village, Dublin 7 (2000)

Arigna Interpretative Centre
Co Leitrim (2003)

Chief O'Neill Hotel
Smithfield Village, Dublin 7 (2000)   230

Old Jameson Distillery Museum
Smithfield Village, Dublin 7 (1998)   232

Hotel in Blanchardstown
Dublin 15 (2008)

6 – A Place for Leisure

Our work demands that we have the utmost respect for context, whether it is a natural landscape or a man-made environment. In the case of the Aillwee Cave Visitor Centre in the Burren, we were working with a magnificently wild and isolated setting – grey limestone hills, constantly shifting clouds and changing light, over-looking a broad expanse of the Atlantic Ocean in the distance. We nestled the building into the rock, fash-ioning it into a rugged and irregular form so that it inte-grated itself into the rocky hill.

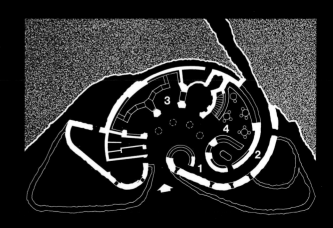

Aillwee Cave Visitor Centre, Co.Clare (1979)

215

Aillwee Cave Visitor Centre

The Aillwee Cave is situated in the Burren, in a wild and unusual landscape created by the grey limestone hills, the Atlantic Ocean and the ever-changing light and clouds. The cave was formed millions of years ago by a great underground river, but it is now dry, and its roof and floor are adorned with magnificent stalactites and stalagmites.

The function of the building is to regulate and control entry to and exit from the cave, display educational materials, accommodate a souvenir shop, snack shop and small restaurant. The main visitors' entrance to the cave is through the building, which is designed internally to appear as though part of the cave; entering it feels like being inside the cave. The access to the cave is by a curved ramp with the educational material displayed along its walls. The retail areas, offices and kitchenette at ground level are formed as alcoves off the main access space. The restaurant at first-floor level is facing an open terrace, with long-distance views of Galway Bay.

The building is nestled into the hill, integrating with the rocks through its irregular and rugged form and the use of weathered local grey limestone, loosely laid in random sizes. From a distance, the building appears nearly indistinguishable from the landscape. The glass in openings has been reduced to a minimum, and openings have been deeply recessed to avoid reflections.

address – Ballyvaughan, Co Clare
design-completion – 1975-1979
area – 430 m²
client – Aillwee Cave Co Ltd
awards – Shannonside Environmental Award, 1979
   – *Plan* Building of the Year Award, 1980
   – Europa Nostra Diploma, 1980 *(for an 'outstanding contribution to the conservational and enhancement of Europe's architectural and natural heritage')*
   – An Taisce, 1981 (commendation)
   – RIAI Triennial Gold Medal 1977-1979 (commendation)

Access from car park
Original perspective drawing

AILLWEE CAVE VISITOR CENTRE

Tea room, with ramped access to the cave in the background

opposite – Detail of selected weathered stones in external wall

Restaurant at 1st floor level

below (bottom to top) – Section, ground and 1st floor plans

1st floor plan (*key:* 12 – Green roof / 14 – Terrace / 15 – Restaurant / 16 – Kitchen / 17 – Void)

Ground-floor plan (*key:* 1 – Tickets / 2 – Ramp to caves / 3 – Shop / 4 – Snacks)

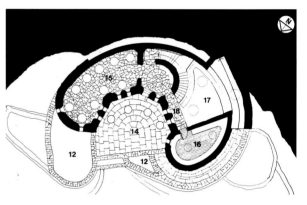

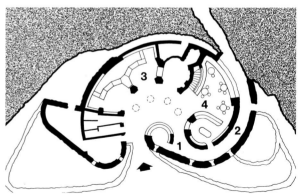

Sports Centre
University College Dublin

The Sports Centre was designed to cater for the recreational needs of the 12,000 students on campus, and to be used for large university functions, such as examinations, conferring and concerts. It consists of two elements – a sports hall and field-games changing areas. A third element, a swimming pool, was designed to adjoin the complex at a later date. The accommodation consists of:

– two large multifunctional halls which can be subdivided with nets for a variety of sports, including tennis, basketball, badminton, netball, judo, archery, fencing and hockey
– six squash courts
– two handball courts
– lounge/viewing area
– table tennis area
– weight-training gymnasium
– administration/seminar rooms
– changing rooms
– equipment store

Retractable seating for 500 spectators is provided in the larger hall. A multitude of galleries in this spacious interior attracts casual spectators to watch games being played, and encourages students to a wider participation in sport.

address – Belfield, Dublin 4
design-completion – 1975-1981
area – 6,800m²
awards – An Taisce Context Award, 1974
– RIAI Triennial Gold Medal, 1980-82 (highly commended)

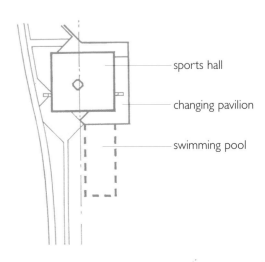

sports hall

changing pavilion

swimming pool

222

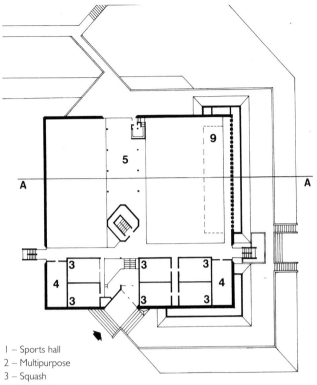

1 – Sports hall
2 – Multipurpose
3 – Squash
4 – Handball
5 – Ping pong
6 – Weights
7 – Changing
8 – Equipment
9 – Moveable seating

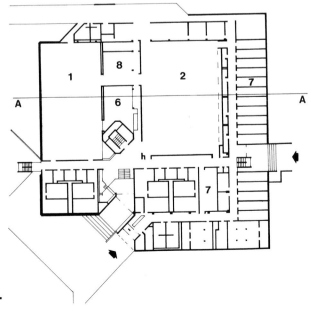

SPORTS CENTRE, UCD

Upper and lower-level plans, and section through 2 multi-functional halls

opposite – View of larger multi-functional hall

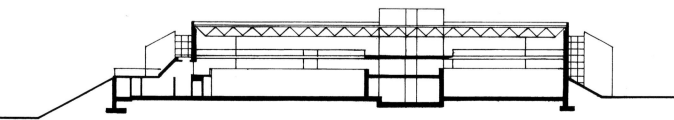

International Hotel in Abu Dhabi – Competition

This hotel required large public spaces for international conferences. The guest rooms are arranged in two blocks, looking towards the sea, and are shaded by forms of overhanging arches. The rooms are opened-up towards the sea through transitional spaces, cooled by shade and wind and enriched with planting and water. The space below the guest-room levels contains all the public rooms, including a conference centre, and steps down towards the sea.

At the end of the gardens, just beside the seashore, there are two swimming pools located on different levels. Gardens are arranged on the rooftops and in various courtyards, so that all major public spaces have a sea view, with luscious vegetation in the foreground. The openings on two sides of the complex, and the voids between the arches at its apex, are designed to allow for maximal wind penetration and cross-ventilation, with shade being maintained most of the time.

The whole complex, seen from the outside, reflects the traditional Islamic simplicity of form of dome and arch, protecting the internal spaces from the sun.

address – Abu Dhabi, United Arab Emirates
design – 1979
area – 44,000m²
competition promoter – International Hotels

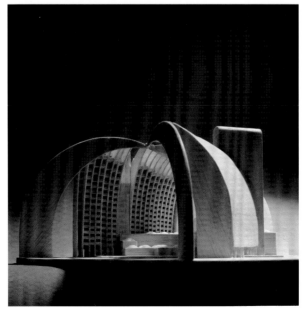

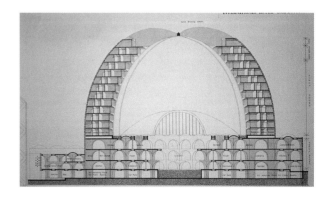

Aquarium in Nouméa
— Competition

We participated in a limited invited competition between five architectural teams from France, Italy and Ireland, run by the EU Environmental Commission, for a new aquarium.

The unique climatic conditions (on the Tropic of Capricorn), and site conditions (on the Pacific coast) would allow an aquarium to be created which was dependent on sunlight and seawater pumped from the Pacific. These are the essential elements for supporting the exquisite local marine flora and fauna, including corals, shallow- and deep-water fish, and the ecosystems of mangroves, lagoons and reefs.

The design concept was based on an elongated, centrally located core of fish tanks, with service and feeding access. Surrounding this was the visitor circulation, which incorporates a variety of zones – land, coast, lagoon, deep sea, barrier reef, islands. The centre core of fish tanks was open to the sunlight and contained photovoltaic panels to provide electrical energy for the visitors' area. An enclosure for visitors was provided in the form of aluminium twin-skin shells, with air-movement in a cavity producing natural cooling.

address – Nouméa, Nouvelle Calédonie
design – 1996
area – 2,650m²
competition promoter – European Union

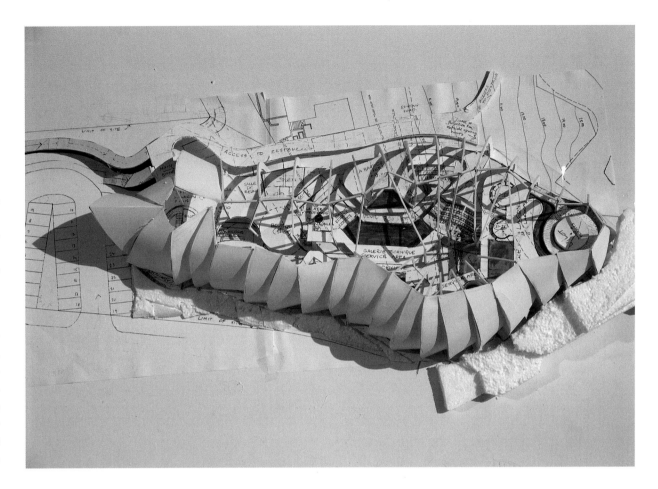

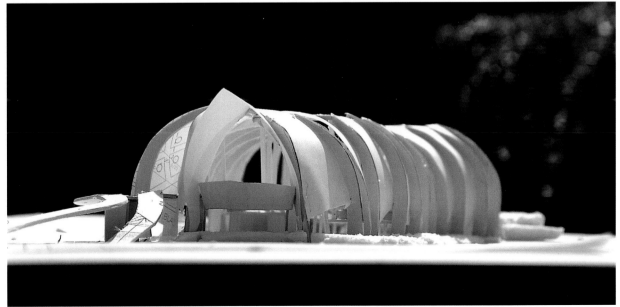

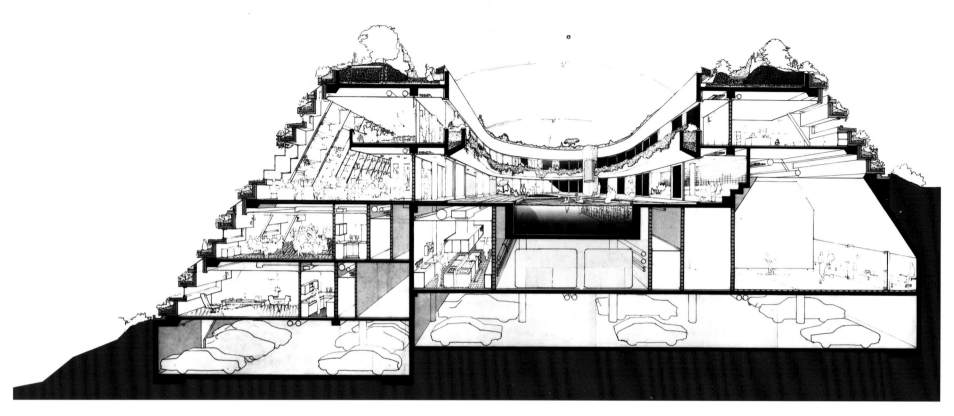

The Peak, Hong Kong
– Competition

The concept for the design of this club and residential complex emanated from the need to balance what is man-made with what is natural in highly populated Hong Kong.

The Peak, like the sea, is an area that should be confined to the natural idiom. Therefore, the plan was conceived as an extension of the hill, with a crater-like internal volume opening to the sky. The crust of this artificial mound is made of containers with earth and planting, and glazed openings. This façade, when planted, will integrate with the surroundings, looking like an overgrown hill rather than a building.

By adopting such an approach, an enlightened example could be set for others to follow, reverting the tendency of developments to pollute this very important natural landmark.

address – The Peak, Hong Kong
design – 1982

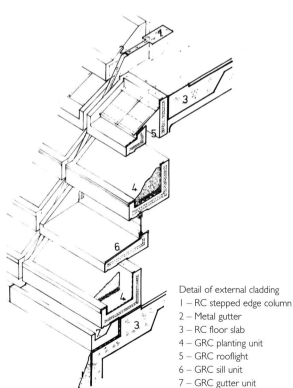

Detail of external cladding
1 – RC stepped edge column
2 – Metal gutter
3 – RC floor slab
4 – GRC planting unit
5 – GRC rooflight
6 – GRC sill unit
7 – GRC gutter unit

Chief O'Neill Hotel
Smithfield Village

The Chief O'Neill Hotel and Ceol Music Centre complex forms part of the much larger Smithfield development. The complex consists of a centre for traditional Irish music and a 74-bedroom hotel. The hotel, with four bedroom floors over public areas, and three attic suites on top, faces Smithfield and wraps itself around the circular drum where the music centre is located. As elsewhere in this development, the existing features from the original distillery site are retained. The powerful brick wall facing Smithfield, which forms an important part of this elevation, is retained, with new openings cut for fenestration. A new semicircular courtyard, in which the original chimney for the observation tower is located, provides an outdoor lobby before entering the hotel.

The interiors of the hotel are light and modern. In the bedrooms, curved etched glass forms the partition of the en-suite bathroom and a freestanding stainless-steel wash-hand basin is installed. The full-height bedhead includes a back-lit glazed panel, etched with musical instruments. All bedrooms are fitted with a CD player, and the artwork is of notable traditional musicians.

Attic suites on the top floor face Smithfield, with a large sunny terrace outside. There is a circular glass bathroom with jacuzzi, and the suites are fitted out to be suitable for meetings as well as living accommodation.

The public spaces are on a number of interconnected levels, with the retained buildings left exposed and colour used selectively.

address – Smithfield, Dublin 7
design-completion – 1995-2000
area – 5,000m²
client – Heritage Properties Ltd; Irish Distillers Group Ltd
awards – Opus Building of the Year Award, 1999
   (commendation)
   – Glen Dimplex Design Award, 1999 (nomination)

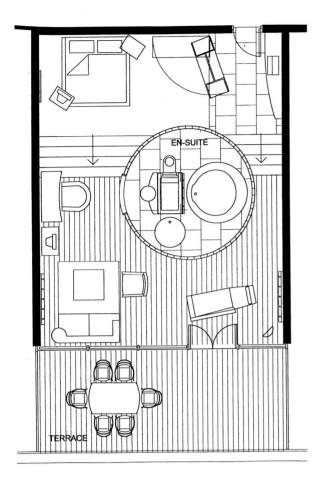

Plan of attic suite

Typical bedroom floor

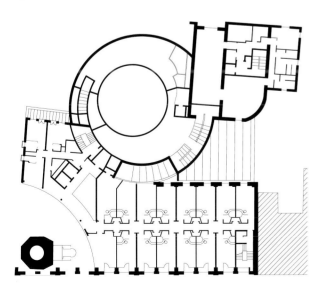

231

Old Jameson Distillery Museum
Smithfield Village

The Old Jameson Distillery faces Bow Street and Church Street New in Smithfield. It is located within the curtilage of Smithfield Village, where John Jameson & Sons once distilled their well-known whiskeys. An audio-visual room introduces visitors to the history of whiskey-making. The exhibition and display area, part of which survives from the 19th-century distillery, demonstrates traditional whiskey-making techniques and processes, and includes a sampling bar.

One aim of the Smithfield Village design is to celebrate its context, both in terms of urban design and building form. This is particularly so in the whiskey centre, where the shape and size of volumes are determined by the original distillery structures. New insertions are intended to be seen as modern, in contrast to the old. The reception area was once filled with vast wash tins of fermenting whiskey, and their bases can still be seen through cut-outs in the floor. Original beams help support the mezzanine, and their size reflects the large loads carried in supporting vats and stills. Brick drums, which were the kiln bases for the stills, serve as the rear wall to the reception. One houses a new stairs and lift and a passage through; the other leads from the audio-visual room to the cantilevered stairs leading to the museum on the first floor. Drying floors and milling rooms are recreated, and visitors pass a working model of a mash tin before entering the still room, with a view over the reception area. A bonded warehouse display, with bottling, barrels and packaging, completes the tour. The resulting jigsaw gives a fair representation of the complexity and ad hoc incremental nature of the original distillery.

address – Smithfield, Dublin 7
design-completion – 1995-1998
area – 3,336m²
client – Heritage Properties Ltd; Irish Distillers Group Ltd
awards – ICAD Annual Awards (bronze award)
in collaboration with Robin Wade & Partners

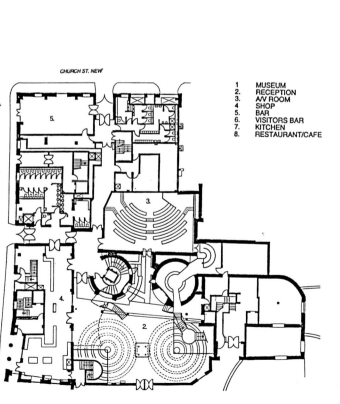

CHURCH ST. NEW

1   MUSEUM
2.   RECEPTION
3.   A/V ROOM
4   SHOP
5.   BAR
6.   VISITORS BAR
7.   KITCHEN
8.   RESTAURANT/CAFE

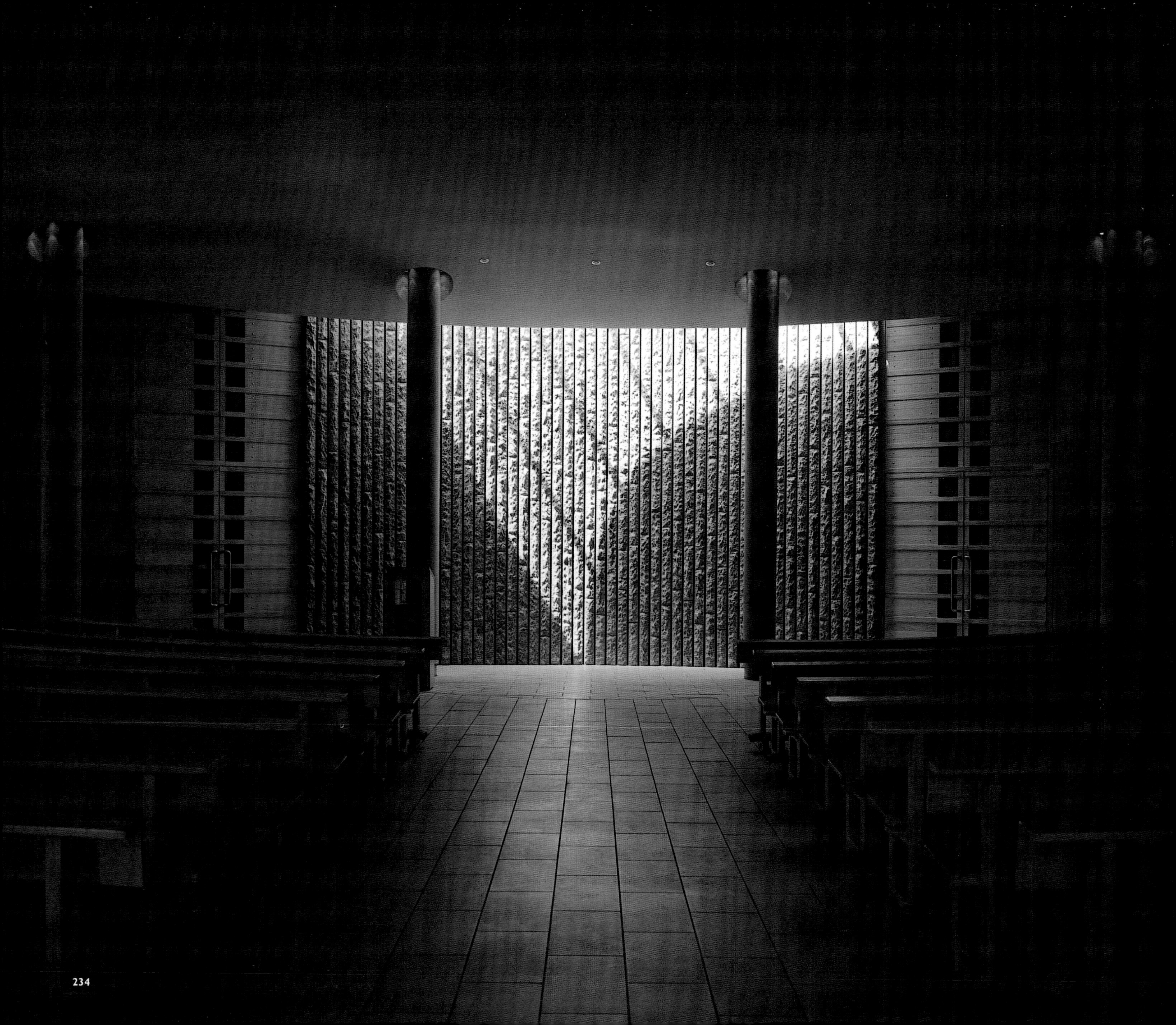

7 – A Place for Culture and Spirituality

National Library, Teheran
– competition (1971)

Holy Trinity Church
Donaghmede, Co Dublin (1978)   page 238

Parish Church
Blessington, Co Wicklow (1982)

Knock Apparition Chapel
Co Mayo (1992)   242

Irish World Heritage Centre
Manchester (1992)

20th-Century Museum, Japan
– Shinkenchiku Competition (1994)   244

Cong Church
Co Mayo (2003)   258

The Helix Performing Arts Centre
Dublin City University (2003)   260

Glasnevin National Heritage Project
Dublin 11 (2009)   270

7 – A Place for Culture and Spirituality

In the buildings reviewed in this group, we have endeavoured to reflect values that move beyond what is currently considered appropriate. As the social order is fast changing, so also are cultural and spiritual values. For example, the main complex at Newlands Cross Cemetery consists of three interlocking pavilions – temple, cloister and administration. The temple will be used for services of all denominations. Instead of using symbols specific to individual religions, we have chosen to express the importance of this place with a universal symbol – light. Around about midday, the sun's rays, directed from the rooflight, create a unique image of light that moves along the wall of the sanctuary and gently touches the floor below.

Newlands Cross Cemetery Buildings, Dublin 22 (2000)

Holy Trinity Church, Donaghmede

The church provides 1,100 seats and incorporates a small chapel and sacristy. The cruciform plan responds to the appropriate relationships between congregation and the area of main liturgical action, establishing short distances from the sanctuary to the furthest seats, easy access by the congregation to the altar, and good sight lines from all seats towards the sanctuary. The low roof profile maintains the human scale of the external perimeter and symbolically rises high above sight lines to the sanctuary area.

Competition assessors' report – *The striking form of this design is a clear expression of the unique structural system used to roof a cruciform plan. The arrangement of voids and solids provides excellent high level lighting to the church.*

address – Donaghmede, Co Dublin
design-completion – 1977-1978
area – 1,028m²
client – Dublin Dioceses

TRINITY TRIANGLES
by Jonathan Glancey

The Holy Trinity is no better represented in architectural terms than through the triangle. Here in Grangemore, Dublin, the Catholic church stridently proclaims the three-in-one Godhead through a severely geometrical structure which expresses very successfully a rational Catholic architecture and an irrational spirituality.

Architects Andrzej and Danuta Wejchert have argued Catholic symbolism through mathematical forms at the same time as creating a cocoon of religious calm inside the church through the use of warm suffused light and the clever pitching of the roofs. Holy Trinity Church dominates its surroundings, acting as a focal point for what is otherwise an uninspired part of suburban Dublin. As the sun sets, it flames on the Trinity-symbol windows as if shining from shook foil.

The cruciform building is sited on a green park and can be seen from all cardinal points of the compass. Through entrances on all four sides it welcomes its congregation from each point of the suburb. As Catholic congregations are still very large, the church is necessarily big, with a floor space of 1,028m² and a total capacity of 1,066 seats, and the whole dramatic tent-like interior is given over to arena seating around a centrally placed altar. The congregation sits on three sides, with good sight lines from all seats towards the sanctuary. It shares closely in the liturgy with the altar no more than 15m from the furthest seat. The low roof lines at the perimeter of the church maintain a comfortable and humane scale for the congregation before soaring symbolically high beyond the sight angle above the sanctuary area.

Behind the altar is a small day chapel on a much homelier scale, and above this, on a first-floor level, are rooms for a variety of parish uses, as well as lavatory facilities. Fan-assisted convector heating warms the winter faithful, while permanent ventilation is provided under and over the high-level glazing in order to avoid condensation. Church furnishings are chaste and simple; indeed, it would be a pity to mar this simple shrine with the kitsch clutter of most central Dublin churches. Altar, chairs and pews are in stained timber, the baptismal font is stone, and the great cross behind the altar is formed by a recess in the concrete block wall separating

the sanctuary from the day chapel. The tabernacle is made of bright metal.

The exciting shape of the church derives from a simple structure. A square steel frame on four stanchions supports roof raking beams, made stable by the provision of a lateral steel brace at the mid-section of the roof walls. The whole steel structure rests on a 100mm reinforced-concrete power-floated slab.

Warm light seeps through huge areas of bronze reflective glass with the rough surface facing outside. As a result, the architect says 'the glass reflects the ever-changing colours of the sky, but it does not reflect the details. Internally it admits soft brown light, and being translucent but not transparent it cuts off rather distractive views out.'

Holy Trinity Church shows clearly that church commissions offer the opportunity of building exciting architecture. In an age that proclaims itself to be rational and systematic and often snubs the sublime, the catholic patronage of the Catholic church is as fresh as the first Christian shrine. The Wejcherts have produced an open, rational and systematic building, but it is one that casts a magic spell. It is an architecture for the Catholic faithful, but also, perhaps, for everyman.

The Architects' Journal, °12, vol. 169, March 1979 (Architectural Press, London, 1979), pp.570-72

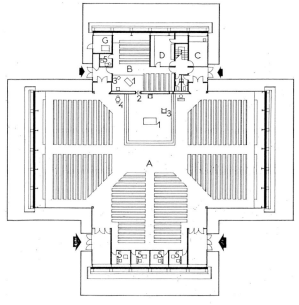

KEY:

A   MAIN CHURCH
B   DAY CHAPEL
C   PRIESTS' VESTRY
D   UTILITY AND ALTAR BOYS' ROOM
E   MEETING ROOM
F   INTERVIEW ROOM
G   BOILER ROOM

1   ALTAR
2   TABERNACLE
3   AMBO
4   BAPTISMAL FONT
5   CONFESSIONALS

HOLY TRINITY CHURCH

Ground-floor plan

Section with view of altar wall

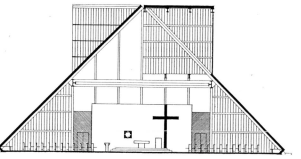

Knock Apparition Chapel

The Apparition Chapel is designed to seat 150 people and to house the tableau depicting the apparition of Our Lady at Knock on 21st August 1879. The chapel reflects the form of the church gable where the apparition took place. It creates a canopy to protect the gable and focus attention on the tableau.

The chapel also acts as a modifier of light by creating a dark frame for the apparition gable while allowing as much light as possible to fall on the tableau. The illumination of the chapel attempts to recreate something of the extraordinary celestial light described by eye-witnesses to the event through the use of natural light and a sophisticated system of lighting controls.

The chapel is constructed of local stone and roofed with a natural stone slate. The gable wall is fully glazed with non-reflective glass to allow unimpeded views of the apparition gable from the entire Knock campus.

address – Our Lady's Shrine, Knock, Co Mayo
design-completion – 1990-1992
area – 325m^2
client – Our Lady's Shrine

Holy water font sculpture by Imogen Stuart

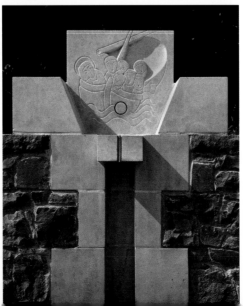

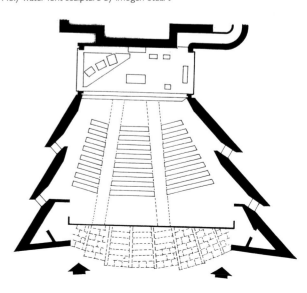

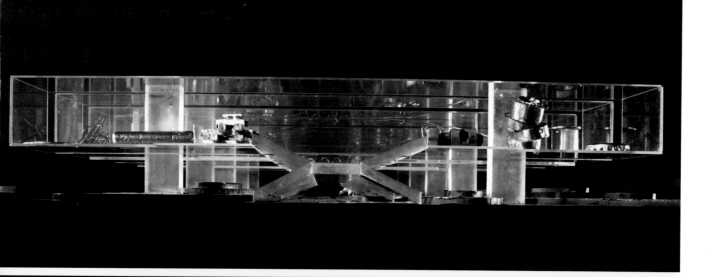

20th-Century Museum
Shinkenchiku Competition

The museum space is organised on three levels. At ground-floor level, the history of mankind is like a river, the rise and fall of democracy, of dictatorship wars, peace, persecution all flowing like many streams, adjoining and mixing in a big river. At this level of the museum, a subject-orientated visit takes place, where one can walk without the constraints of time, guided by events forming a history.

The top level divides the time into ten sections. Each contains a decade. Separate, often unconnected discoveries, inventions or creations within each decade are marked and explained. It could be the first performance of the *Sacre du Printemps* by Igor Stravinsky (1913) or man's first step on the moon (1969). These are products of the human mind, like stars shining, singly isolated, floating above humanity.

The lowest level, below ground, contains access to research facilities, audio-visual and library material.

The visual connectivity and transparency between all levels will be secured by glass floors. Escalators would allow for continuous movement between the three levels within each decade.

address – Japan
design – 1994
area – 50,000m²

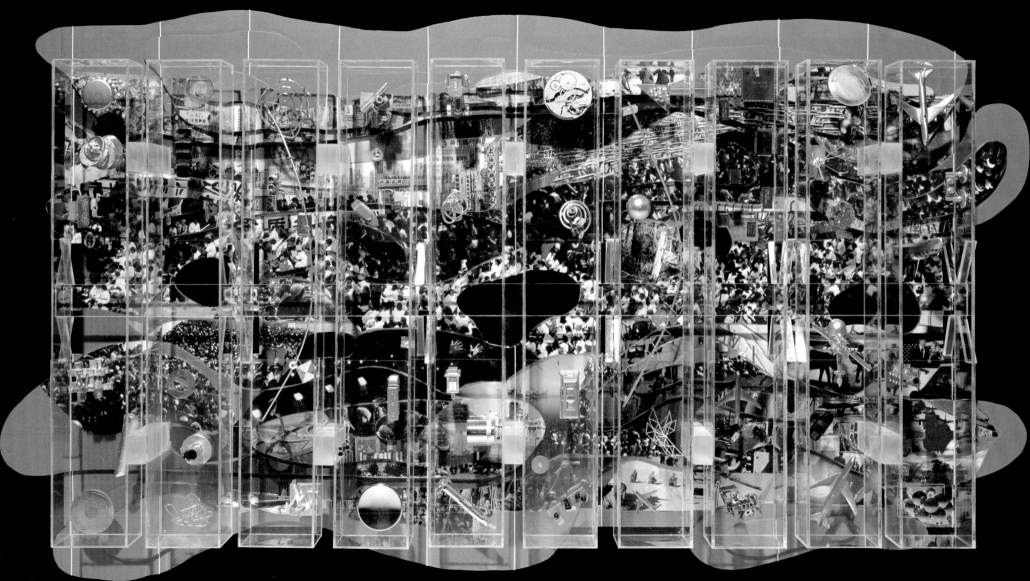

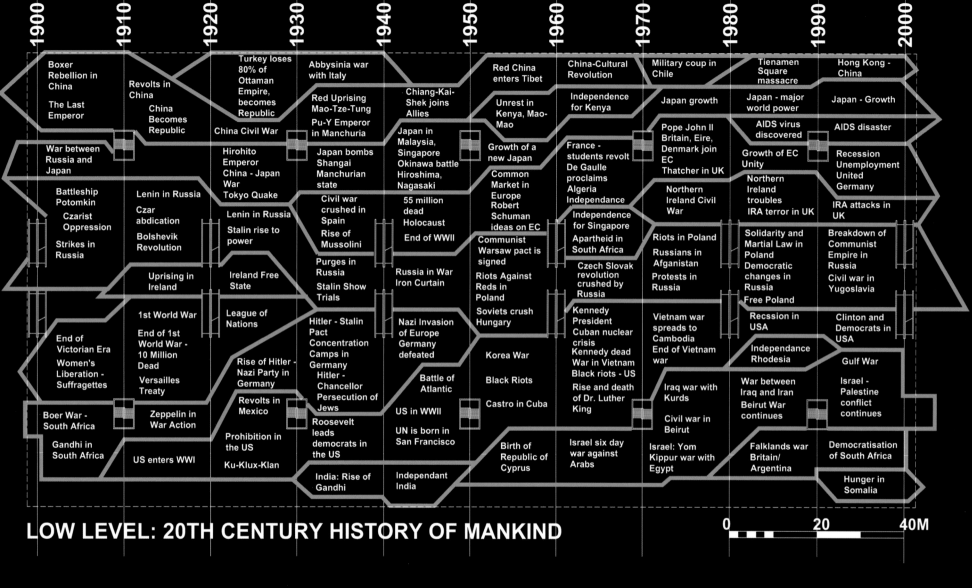

| 1900 | 1910 | 1920 | 1930 | 1940 | 1950 | 1960 | 1970 | 1980 | 1990 | 2000 |

Boxer Rebellion in China

The Last Emperor

Revolts in China

China Becomes Republic

Turkey loses 80% of Ottaman Empire, becomes Republic

China Civil War

Abbysinia war with Italy

Red Uprising Mao-Tze-Tung

Pu-Y Emperor in Manchuria

Chiang-Kai-Shek joins Allies

Japan in Malaysia, Singapore Okinawa battle Hiroshima, Nagasaki

Red China enters Tibet

Unrest in Kenya, Mao-Mao

Growth of a new Japan

China-Cultural Revolution

Independence for Kenya

Military coup in Chile

Japan growth

Tienamen Square massacre

Japan - major world power

AIDS virus discovered

Hong Kong - China

Japan - Growth

AIDS disaster

War between Russia and Japan

Battleship Potomkin

Czarist Oppression

Strikes in Russia

Lenin in Russia

Czar abdication

Bolshevik Revolution

Hirohito Emperor China - Japan War Tokyo Quake

Lenin in Russia

Stalin rise to power

Japan bombs Shangai Manchurian state

Civil war crushed in Spain

Rise of Mussolini

55 million dead Holocaust

End of WWII

Russia in War Iron Curtain

France - students revolt De Gaulle proclaims Algeria Independance

Independence for Singapore

Apartheid in South Africa

Pope John II Britain, Eire, Denmark join EC

Thatcher in UK

Northern Ireland Civil War

Growth of EC Unity

Northern Ireland troubles

IRA terror in UK

Recession Unemployment United Germany

IRA attacks in UK

End of Victorian Era

Women's Liberation - Suffragettes

Uprising in Ireland

1st World War

End of 1st World War - 10 Million Dead

Versailles Treaty

Ireland Free State

League of Nations

Purges in Russia

Stalin Show Trials

Hitler - Stalin Pact Concentration Camps in Germany Hitler - Chancellor Persecution of Jews

Nazi Invasion of Europe Germany defeated

Battle of Atlantic

Communist Warsaw pact is signed

Riots Against Reds in Poland

Soviets crush Hungary

Korea War

Czech Slovak revolution crushed by Russia

Kennedy President Cuban nuclear crisis Kennedy dead War in Vietnam Black riots - US

Riots in Poland

Russians in Afganistan

Protests in Russia

Vietnam war spreads to Cambodia End of Vietnam war

Solidarity and Martial Law in Poland Democratic changes in Russia

Free Poland

Recssion in USA

Independance Rhodesia

Breakdown of Communist Empire in Russia

Civil war in Yugoslavia

Clinton and Democrats in USA

Gulf War

Boer War - South Africa

Gandhi in South Africa

Zeppelin in War Action

US enters WWI

Rise of Hitler - Nazi Party in Germany

Revolts in Mexico

Prohibition in the US

Ku-Klux-Klan

Roosevelt leads democrats in the US

India: Rise of Gandhi

US in WWII

UN is born in San Francisco

Independant India

Black Riots

Castro in Cuba

Birth of Republic of Cyprus

Rise and death of Dr. Luther King

Israel six day war against Arabs

Iraq war with Kurds

Civil war in Beirut

Israel: Yom Kippur war with Egypt

War between Iraq and Iran Beirut War continues

Falklands war Britain/ Argentina

Israel - Palestine conflict continues

Democratisation of South Africa

Hunger in Somalia

LOW LEVEL: 20TH CENTURY HISTORY OF MANKIND

0   20   40M

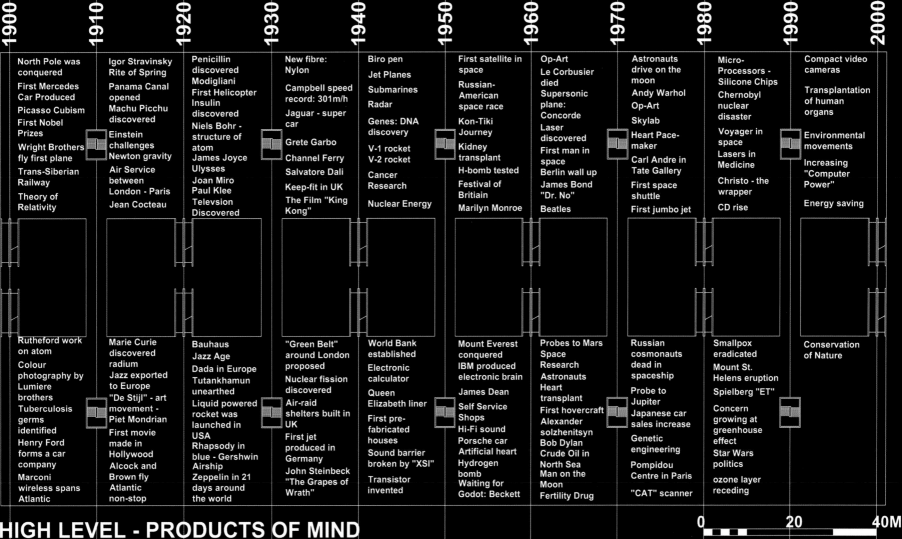

1900	1910	1920	1930	1940	1950	1960	1970	1980	1990	2000
North Pole was conquered	Igor Stravinsky Rite of Spring	Penicillin discovered	New fibre: Nylon	Biro pen	First satellite in space	Op-Art	Astronauts drive on the moon	Micro-Processors - Silicone Chips	Compact video cameras	
First Mercedes Car Produced	Panama Canal opened	Modigliani		Jet Planes	Russian-American space race	Le Corbusier died	Andy Warhol	Chernobyl nuclear disaster	Transplantation of human organs	
Picasso Cubism	Machu Picchu discovered	First Helicopter	Campbell speed record: 301m/h	Submarines		Supersonic plane: Concorde	Op-Art			
First Nobel Prizes		Insulin discovered		Radar	Kon-Tiki Journey		Skylab	Voyager in space	Environmental movements	
Wright Brothers fly first plane	Einstein challenges Newton gravity	Niels Bohr - structure of atom	Jaguar - super car	Genes: DNA discovery	Kidney transplant	Laser discovered	Heart Pace-maker	Lasers in Medicine	Increasing "Computer Power"	
Trans-Siberian Railway	Air Service between London - Paris	James Joyce Ulysses	Grete Garbo	V-1 rocket V-2 rocket	H-bomb tested	First man in space	Carl Andre in Tate Gallery	Christo - the wrapper		
Theory of Relativity	Jean Cocteau	Joan Miro Paul Klee	Channel Ferry	Cancer Research	Festival of Britiain	Berlin wall up	First space shuttle	CD rise	Energy saving	
		Televsion Discovered	Salvatore Dali	Nuclear Energy	Marilyn Monroe	James Bond "Dr. No"	First jumbo jet			
			Keep-fit in UK			Beatles				
			The Film "King Kong"							
Rutheford work on atom	Marie Curie discovered radium	Bauhaus	"Green Belt" around London proposed	World Bank established	Mount Everest conquered	Probes to Mars	Russian cosmonauts dead in spaceship	Smallpox eradicated	Conservation of Nature	
Colour photography by Lumiere brothers	Jazz exported to Europe	Jazz Age	Nuclear fission discovered	Electronic calculator	IBM produced electronic brain	Space Research		Mount St. Helens eruption		
Tuberculosis germs identified	"De Stijl" - art movement - Piet Mondrian	Dada in Europe	Air-raid shelters built in UK	Queen Elizabeth liner	James Dean	Astronauts Heart transplant	Probe to Jupiter	Spielberg "ET"		
Henry Ford forms a car company	First movie made in Hollywood	Tutankhamun unearthed	First jet produced in Germany	First pre-fabricated houses	Self Service Shops	First hovercraft	Japanese car sales increase	Concern growing at greenhouse effect		
Marconi wireless spans Atlantic	Alcock and Brown fly Atlantic non-stop	Liquid powered rocket was launched in USA	John Steinbeck "The Grapes of Wrath"	Sound barrier broken by "XSI"	Hi-Fi sound	Alexander solzhenitsyn	Genetic engineering	Star Wars politics		
		Rhapsody in blue - Gershwin		Transistor invented	Porsche car	Bob Dylan	Pompidou Centre in Paris	ozone layer receding		
		Airship Zeppelin in 21 days around the world			Artificial heart	Crude Oil in North Sea	"CAT" scanner			
					Hydrogen bomb	Man on the Moon				
					Waiting for Godot: Beckett	Fertility Drug				

HIGH LEVEL - PRODUCTS OF MIND

0   20   40M

Newlands Cross
Cemetery Buildings

The main building complex consists of three interlocking pavilions surrounded by gardens – the Temple Building, which contains the main space for burial rites; a circular cloistered meeting ring (the broken ring symbolises man's finite time span), and an administration building. This complex was designed following a distinct spatial sequence from arrival, through the buildings and gardens, towards the burial plots.

IRISH ARCHITECTURE AWARD, 2001

Citation – *A well-constructed plan following a distinct spatial sequence. Stone, metal and light are well used to give gravitas and restfulness.*

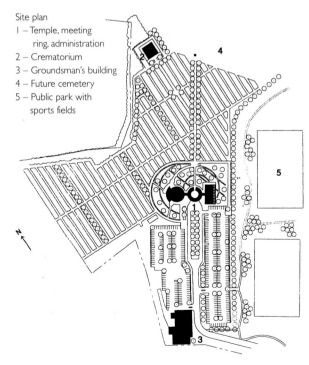

Site plan
1 – Temple, meeting
    ring, administration
2 – Crematorium
3 – Groundsman's building
4 – Future cemetery
5 – Public park with
    sports fields

Section and plan
1 – Temple
2 – Meeting ring and pool
3 – Administration

Client's comments – Dublin Cemeteries Committee, a statutory body, charity and non-profit-making organisation, whose roots go back to Daniel O'Connell's Catholic Association in 1829, consecrated the first Catholic burial ground to be established since the inception of the penal laws. The Dublin Cemeteries Committee is multi-denominational, reflecting O'Connell's express wish that no religion or sect be excluded, and ensuring that religious diversity is kept alive to this day.

The Committee's most recent developments are Newlands Cross Cemetery in 2000 and Newlands Cross Crematorium in 2001. Newlands Cross is the first cemetery to be designed in an existing parkland landscape since the close of the Victorian era, when cemeteries like the Glasgow Necropolis, City of London, Père Lachaise and Glasnevin were designed and developed.

A multidiscipline design and construction team of landscape architects, architects, civil and structural engineers, hydrologists, project managers and park superintendents was put in place from the outset. The buildings at Newlands consist of a temple

building to be used for crematorium services, a beautiful fountain and cloistered meeting area, administration building and crematorium, all harmoniously interconnected and integrated into the existing landscape by use of extensive planting of mature and semi-mature native indigenous plants. The project demonstrates the commitment by the Dublin Cemeteries Committee to providing burial and crematorium services to the city and county of Dublin for the next century and beyond.

address – Dublin 22
design-completion –1998-2000
area – 1,722 m²
client – Dublin Cemeteries Committee
awards – RIAI Regional Award, 2001
    – Opus Building of the Year Award (highly commended)

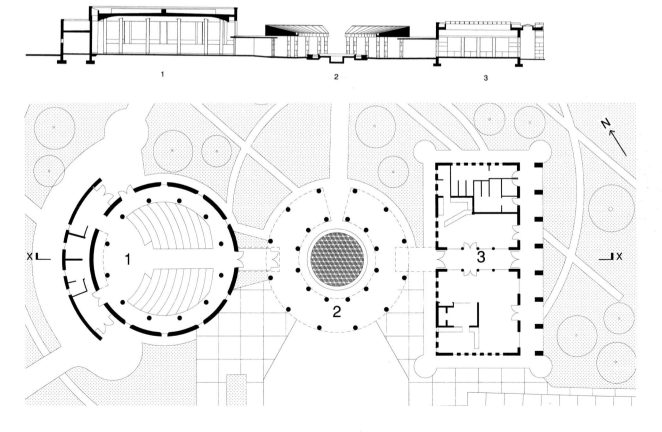

NEWLANDS CROSS CEMETERY BUILDINGS

Entrance to temple

opposite

Detail of temple interior

Administration building

Stonework detail

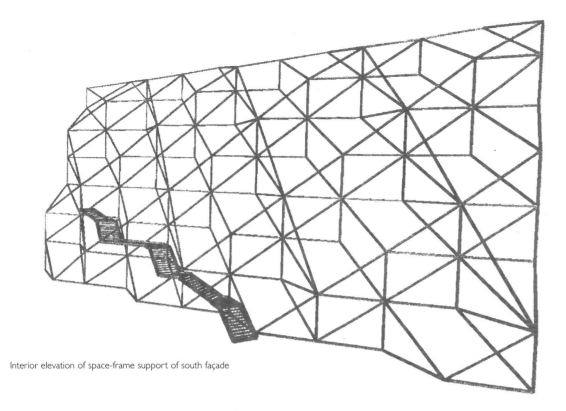

Interior elevation of space-frame support of south façade

North Quay Venue Building – Competition

The Venue Building is located at the eastern end of the Waterford North Quay development. It will act as a gateway to Waterford in the approach from the east along the river, and as an anchor for the entire North Quay development in the approach from the west. It is appropriate that, as a first phase, the Venue Building will be used as a strong attraction for other developments owing to its scale and image.

In contrast to the introverted nature of the auditorium, the foyer will become the main space to correspond with its surroundings. From within the multi-level glazed foyer space, people will have a panoramic view of the city and river, with passing boats.

The views from the south quays and the river towards the foyer will reveal a space animated by visitors' movement and electronic display projections. Above all, the foyer's glazed, multifaceted Cartesian wall as a crystalline structure will reflect every change of weather and movement of water, acting as a virtual screen on a scale and quality unseen before.

address – North Quay, Waterford
design – 2002
area – 5,600m²
competition promoter – Office of Public Works

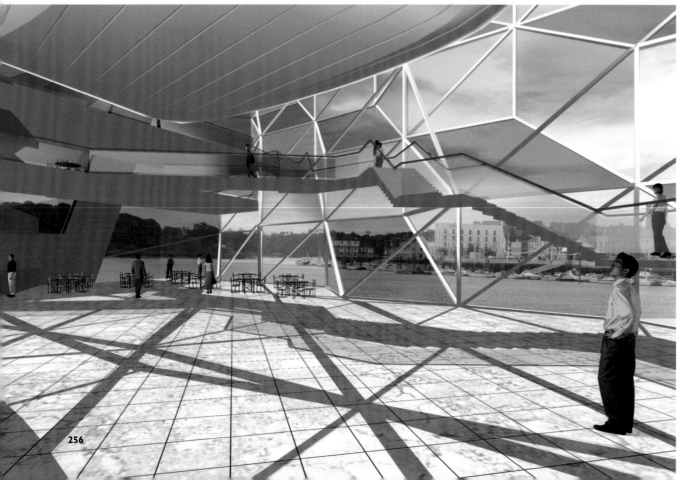

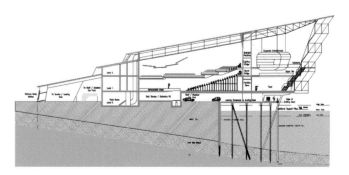

256

Cong Church

This project involved the extensive refurbishing and part rebuilding of a church that was built in 1973, which, in turn, had replaced a 19th-century church. The work included a new limestone exterior with patinated bronze cross and entrance arch, limed oak joinery and patinated zinc roofing and walling. The internal remodelling involved raising the ceiling height over the main body of the church. The church adjoins the 12th-century Cong Abbey ruin.

address – Cong, Co Mayo
design-completion – 2000-2003
area – 400m²
client – Fr Colm Kilcoyne

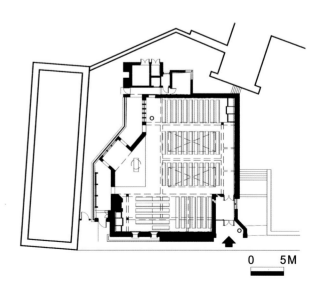

0   5M

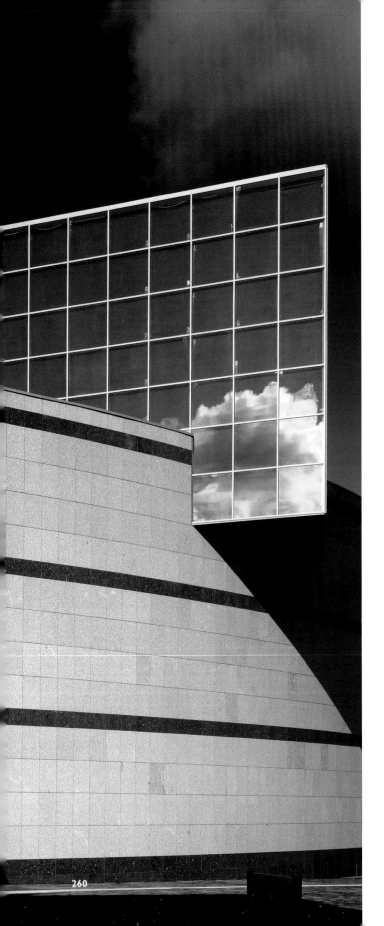

The Helix
Performing Arts Centre
Dublin City University

This multidisciplinary centre for music, drama and visual arts includes a 1,250-seat aula maxima/concert hall, a 450-seat theatre and a 150-seat studio theatre, with exhibition space, backstage and ancillary areas. The three auditoria are grouped around the central foyer, which serves all levels and is linked by voids and freestanding staircases. Externally the building is clad in pale-grey granite elements and black granite. Its volume and scale set it apart from the academic buildings and the stone and glass are chosen to provide a contrast without dominating the adjacent buildings.

The most essential condition for the success of such a centre is an ability to change and adapt to a variety of diverse uses. At the Helix, due to the major technological features provided, the seating layouts and ratio of audience to performance can be changed to allow for alternative uses, ranging from theatre, cinema and concerts to exhibitions, banquets, examinations and conferences.

Location – The Helix faces the main campus entrance from Collins Avenue in a buffer zone between the academic core and the community. A ceremonial entrance takes advantage of the slope across the site. The entrance and multistorey glazed foyer provide visitors with an open, welcoming appearance. The façade adjoining the campus conforms to the campus axis, while the gentle curve facing the access directs the general pedestrian traffic flow towards the central campus mall The curved form of the building relates to the circular form of the Larkin Theatre directly opposite the site, and as such forms a gentle threshold to the academic buildings beyond. The building is easily accessible from the adjoining multistorey car park at ground level or through an underground tunnel link. Service traffic and deliveries are directed to the west end of the site, with a service road situated between the new building and the Henry Grattan Building.

Space organisation: the foyer – The space is organised by a

dynamic geometry derived from three axis converging in the foyer, around which are organised the three major theatre spaces. The foyer, as the main organising space in the building, is arranged over three levels with an interconnecting open void, through which light spills from the roof. The void has a series of sweeping stairways to invite patrons to the upper levels. This is the focus of the building, with spaces opening directly off this central node.

O'Mahony Concert Hall / Aula Maxima – This is the largest performance space in the building, arranged over two levels with capacity for 1,250 people. The space was designed for a variety of functions, and can be used with a flat floor or with raked seating. Its prime use as a concert hall directed the design towards excellence in acoustics. The high volume of 20m was combined with a traditional 'shoe box' layout, acknowledged internationally for excellent acoustics. At ground-floor level, there is a large bank of retractable seating as well as removable flat-floor seating in front of the stage. At the upper level there is sweeping series of balconies, which step down towards the stage.

Theatre and studio theatre – The main theatre has an audience capacity of 450. It is designed on the model of a proscenium arch theatre, suitable for most types of theatrical productions. The orchestra pit can be converted into a fore-stage area, which, together with the curved side walls of the auditoria, will allow a thrust type stage to be formed.

address – Dublin 9
design-completion – 1997-2003
area – 11,650m²
client – Dublin City University
awards – Irish Concrete Society Award, 2003
    – Irish Joinery Award, 2003
    – Opus Building of the Year Award, 2003
    Citation – *This building is symbolically and physically the public face of Dublin City University, located as it is between the public street and the private campus. The three key elements of concert hall, theatre and studio theatre are architecturally held together by their respective axes which interlink in the entrance foyer. Their dynamic geometry is counterpointed by the calm of their respective interiors, where assured detailing ensures focussed calmness and good acoustics.*

The Helix
by Marie-Louise O'Donnell

Performance spaces are where something happens; they are where people go to be entertained, awed, moved, inspired, and sometimes even changed or altered by what they see and hear. They are where actors, musicians and performers play, and the audience gets caught up in the play in the happening.

The Helix is a building of great beauty. It is itself a performance, a happening. Built in a sweeping curvilinear of silver-grey stone and glass, it is magnificent to look at, to walk around, amble past, or simply observe from a distance. It sits quietly dominant like two great rounded stone urns brought together by a large glass-fronted entrance, which overlooks a large open courtyard space and a car park that is connected to its entrance by an underground link. The silver-grey smooth curve of the walls, and the long, wide glass windows that wrap themselves around the building invite you to stop and look, and your eyes are taken on a gentle journey around the arc and turn of the building, and are raised up towards the external flytower of the main Theatre – a unique flytower that emerges from the circular stone like a giant magic box high in the sky, a glass box that is cut finely and sharply into the building, through which the clouds are reflected during the day, and which becomes a glowing iridescent crystal box at night.

The expansive, circular, bright foyers arranged on all three floors set the tone, atmosphere and a feeling of invitation. Once inside this building you know immediately that you are about to experience something alive and interesting. Three performance spaces sit gently and discreetly around the arc of the ground floor foyer – a concert hall, a theatre and a studio theatre. They are finely placed, finely integrated, and an outstanding addition to the performing arts in Ireland.

Irish Arts Review, vol. 19, °3, winter 2002, pp.90-97. Marie-Louise O'Donnell is Artistic Programmer at The Helix.

2nd and ground-floor plans and section

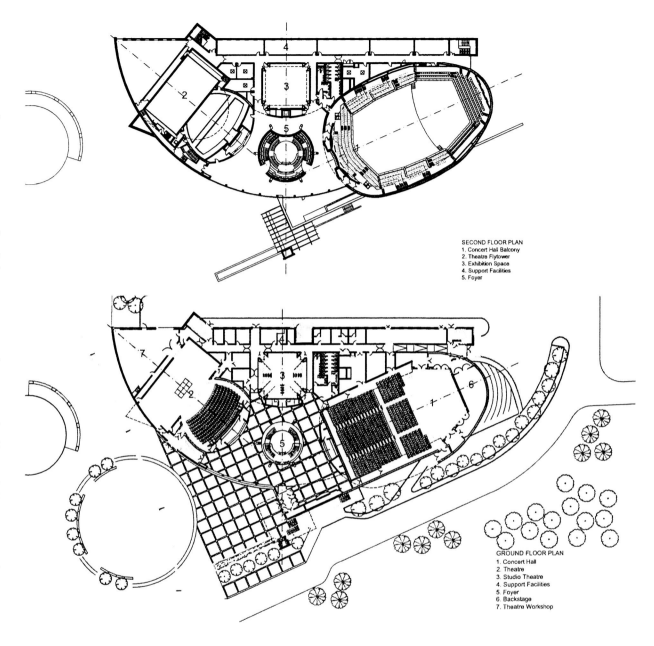

SECOND FLOOR PLAN
1. Concert Hall Balcony
2. Theatre Flytower
3. Exhibition Space
4. Support Facilities
5. Foyer

GROUND FLOOR PLAN
1. Concert Hall
2. Theatre
3. Studio Theatre
4. Support Facilities
5. Foyer
6. Backstage
7. Theatre Workshop

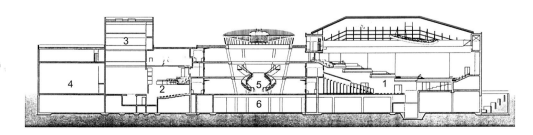

SECTION
1. Concert Hall
2. Theatre
3. Theatre Flytower
4. Theatre Workshop
5. Foyer
6. Plantrooms / Technical Facilitie

Glasnevin National Heritage Project

Glasnevin Cemetery is run by the Dublin Cemeteries Committee, which is a successor to the committee founded by Daniel O'Connell in 1828. The Committee plans to expand the amenity potential of the cemetery by presenting the cemetery's history in its national context.

The Committee identified the need for a new building near the entrance to the cemetery, which would present in visual form the history of the cemetery and the achievements of those who are buried there.

The Daniel O'Connell Tower became a central point of reference in the composition. The new entrance area, its hard landscape, pavements and the new Heritage Building, are organised along lines radiating from the tower.

The space for the Heritage Building is contained between the existing boundary wall and the new perforated curved wall. This wall points at one end towards the O'Connell Tower and embraces the adjoining graves, integrated now into the overall composition. The roof over this space floats like a cloud.

address – Glasnevin, Dublin 11
design-completion – 2007-2009
area – 2,000m²
client – Dublin Cemeteries Committee

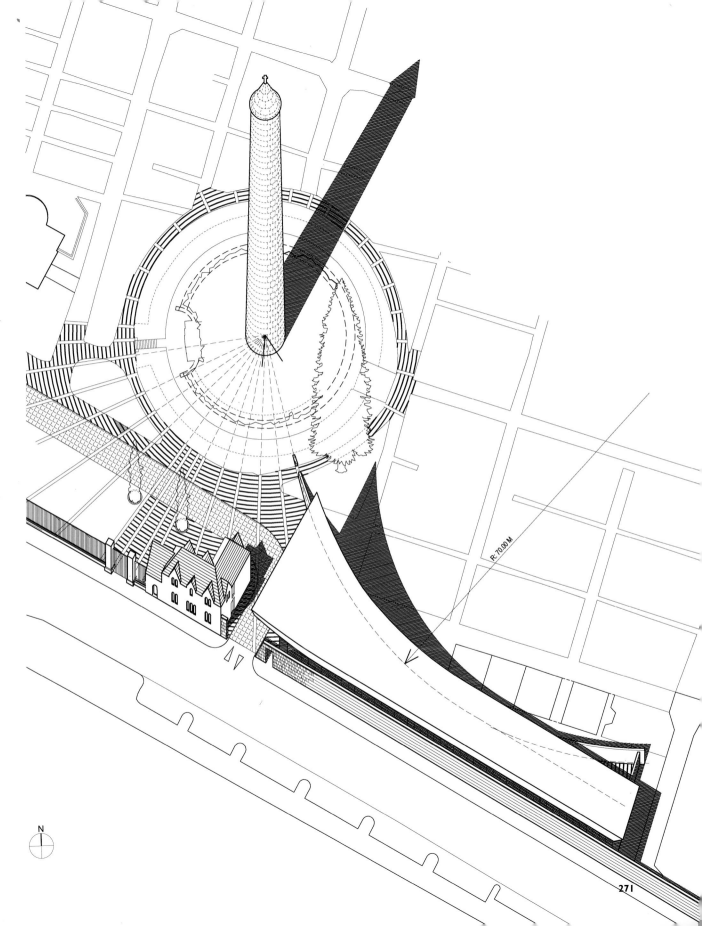

271

The Practice

IN 1964 ANDRZEJ WEJCHERT COMMENCED ARCHITECTURAL PRACTICE IN IRELAND ON THE strength of the winning entry in the international architectural competition for the master plan for the new campus and Arts, Administration and Aula Maxima buildings for University College Dublin. During the development stage of this project, Andrzej Wejchert worked with Robinson Keefe Devane, Associate Architects.

In 1974, with Danuta Kornaus-Wejchert, he established the partnership of A&D Wejchert Architects. At the beginning the work concentrated on educational projects. Following numerous architectural competitions the scope of the work widened to include healthcare, commercial and sacral architecture.

Over the years, Patrick Fletcher, Martin Carey, Paul Roche, Helen Giblin, David Lanigan and Graham Dwyer joined the practice and become partners. Hugh Maguire, Keith Meagan and Wade Sutton became associates. Subsequently (in 1999) the practice name became A&D Wejchert & Partners. The practice ethos is similar to that of a family, where work and challenges are shared between all.

The practice is registered with the Royal Institute of the Architects of Ireland.

Extension to offices at 23 Lower Baggot Street

Partners, Associates, Staff

ANDRZEJ WEJCHERT

Andrzej Wejchert graduated from the Faculty of Architecture at Warsaw Polytechnic. While working in the municipal design office for city buildings in Warsaw, he participated in various architectural competitions. In 1964 he won the international architectural competition for the master plan for the new campus and Arts, Administration and Aula Maxima buildings for University College, Dublin. In 1974, with Danuta Kornaus-Wejchert, he co-founded the practice of A&D Wejchert Architects in Dublin. Their work initially concentrated on buildings for education, ranging from schools to universities. Andrzej Wejchert was awarded the RIAI Triennial Gold Medal, 1971-73, for the Administration Building at UCD. His expertise in development planning led to commissions for technological, business and science parks. In 1985 the practice started a 'long term' engagement with the largest retail project in Ireland at the time – the Blanchardstown Town Centre. The first phase was opened in 1996, and the next phases are still following. In the 1980s Andrzej Wejchert undertook architectural commissions in Poland. The most important were the Media Business Centre and the Sobanski Palace Complex, both in Warsaw. In tandem with work in Ireland, he continues to design buildings in Poland. Andrzej Wejchert also taught architecture at UCD School of Architecture. In 1997 he received an honorary Doctor of Law degree from the National University of Ireland. He is a Fellow of the Royal Institute of the Architects of Ireland (RIAI), a member of the Association of Polish Architects and of the Royal Institute of British Architects (RIBA). He has been twice vice-president of the RIAI, a council member for sixteen years, and is a member of the Professional Conduct Committee. He is a member of the Royal Hibernian Academy and was recently appointed to the board of governors of the National Gallery of Ireland.

DANUTA KORNAUS-WEJCHERT

Danuta Kornaus-Wejchert graduated from Faculty of Architecture at Warsaw Polytechnic, and also studied architecture at the l'École Nationale Supérieure des Beaux-Arts in Paris. During the 1960s she worked in the design office of the Department of Health in Warsaw, with Agence Auffret in Paris, and with Robinson Keefe Devane in Dublin. In 1974 she co-founded, with Andrzej Wejchert, the practice of A&D Wejchert Architects in Dublin. Over the years she has participated in numerous international and national architectural competitions, including the headquarters for the International Organisations and Conference Centre in Vienna; Universita degli Studi della Calabria, Italy; International Hotel in Abu Dhabi, UAE; Aquarium in Nouméa, Nouvelle Calédonie; and Singapore Science Park. Success in a series of architectural competitions including the International Timber Architectural Awards, the Irish Business / Abbey Homestead Housing Awards, and the Dublin Diocesan Church Competition resulted in future commissions for the practice. Participation in the Tallaght Hospital competition led to a long-term engagement with healthcare architecture, from large health projects such as Naas General Hospital and Connolly Hospital at Blanchardstown to smaller health centres and a recent remedial clinic. She is a Fellow of the RIAI, a member of the Association of Polish Architects and of the RIBA.

PATRICK FLETCHER

Patrick Fletcher graduated from University College Dublin (UCD) School of Architecture in 1975. He joined A&D Wejchert Architects in 1975, was made an associate in 1984 and a partner in 1999. His work has mostly been related to educational and commercial buildings, as well as a number of private houses. His main interests are sustainability and low-energy design, and he was a partner-in-charge of the Waterford Institute of Technology library, which won the Minister for the Environment's Sustainability 2000 Award. Among the projects for which he is responsible are Beresford Court for Irish Life; offices for Irish Cement; O'Rahilly Building, UCC; library, IT building, canteen and Nurse Education Building for Waterford Institute of Technology; the Robert Schuman and Kathleen Lonsdale Buildings for the University of Limerick; and community schools at Brookfield, Tallaght, Youghal and Castleknock. He is a Fellow of the RIAI and a member of its Competence Task Force. He is also a member of the RIBA.

MARTIN CAREY

Martin Carey graduated from UCD School of Architecture in 1977 and has worked with this practice since then. He became an associate in 1984 and a partner in 1999. While principally involved in the design and construction of buildings over the years, he has developed an interest and expertise in master-planning and management, notably in science and technology parks in Poland, Turkey and Singapore. This expertise has been employed in hospital development control plans, including Naas General Hospital, Letterkenny General Hospital, Sligo General Hospital and the Connolly Hospital in Blanchardstown. He has also handled a number of the firm's sacral projects, inducing the Apparition Chapel in Knock and Blessington Church. He is a Fellow of the RIAI and a member of the RIBA.

PAUL ROCHE

Paul Roche graduated from the School of Architecture, Dublin Institute of Technology in 1981, and has been with A&D Wejchert & Partners since 1974. He became an associate in 1984 and a partner in 1999. He has extensive experience in the design of retail and commercial buildings and master-planning. He has handled the development of the Blanchardstown Centre from its inception in 1984 to its current phase, including the recent Red Mall extension and retail parks, and the Atrium and Q office buildings on peripheral sites. His other projects include the office building at 65-66 Lower Mount Street, government offices in Letterkenny, and the new Gaiety Centre project in Dublin. He has also been responsible for one-off house-design projects, such as Heather Cottage on Howth Head. He has built a reputation for successfully handling large complex projects together with understanding and integrat-

ing clients' needs into the building design. He is a member of the RIAI and of the RIBA.

HELEN GIBLIN

Helen Giblin graduated from UCD School of Architecture in 1977. She also has a diploma in Project Management from Trinity College Dublin. She joined A&D Wejchert Architects in 1981, where she worked on the award-winning AnCo Training Centre at Loughlinstown, after working initially in Edinburgh for Basil Spence Glover & Ferguson. Subsequently she worked in Ireland, the UK and Boston before returning to A&D Wejchert in 1995. She became an associate in 1997 and a partner in 1999. She was project architect on Smithfield Village, an innovative inner-city mixed-use development. She has a particular interest in urban design and in integrating old with new, as in Smithfield Village, and is the partner in charge of the practice's conservation accreditation. She also has expertise in healthcare, and is familiar with all aspects, both primary and acute. She was project architect on the development at Connolly Hospital, Blanchardstown. She is a member of the Royal Institute of Architects of Ireland and the American Institute of Architects.

DAVID LANIGAN

David Lanigan graduated from UCD School of Architecture in 1986, and has been with the practice since 1990. He became an associate in 1997 and a partner in 1999. He worked in London for a number of years for respected architects, including Nicholas Lacey Jobst & Hyett, before returning to Dublin to join the firm. David has a particular interest in public buildings and how the experience of people using them can be enhanced.

His projects have included the award-winning Helix Performing Arts Centre in Dublin City University. He has wide experience in a variety of building types including the Student Centre at UCC and healthcare buildings, including health centres in Swords, Ballymun and Brookfield in Dublin. He has also handled a number of projects abroad, including the Sobanski Palace office building in Poland and the Irish World Heritage Centre in Manchester. Latterly he is involved with major master-planning and urban-design projects and large-scale commercial, mixed-use projects. He is a member of the RIAI, and a member of its Safety Health and Welfare Taskforce. He leads the practice's health and safety services.

GRAHAM DWYER

Graham Dwyer graduated with an honours B.Arch.Sc degree from the National University of Ireland, and a diploma in architecture from Dublin Institute of Technology in 1997. He is currently completing a Masters degree in Urban Design at UCD. He joined A&D Wejchert & Partners in 2001, having worked with a number of prominent architectural practices in Dublin. He became an associate in 2003 and a partner in 2006. Graham has a particular interest in design and 3D visualisation, including presentation graphics, photomontage and daylight and sunlight analysis, and is expert in utilising the latest computer technology in architectural design. He is also involved in master-planning and urban design. His projects include the UCD Development Plan; the Red Mall and Yellow Mall at Blanchardstown Shopping Centre; a retail and office development at South King Street, Dublin. He has also participated in various architectural design competitions, including the Waterford North Quays competition, and the Irish World Performing Arts Village at the University of Limerick, among others. He has been an associate member of the Royal Institute of Architects of Ireland since 1998 and a full member since 2001.

____

ASSOCIATES

HUGH MAGUIRE

Hugh Maguire graduated as an architect with a diploma in architecture from the Faculty of Architecture, Dublin Institute of Technology, and with a B.Arch.Sc from Dublin University (TCD) in 1978. After working with Scott Tallon Walker Architects in Dublin and London, he joined A&D Wejchert in 1987, where he was made an associate in 2000. Among the projects for which he was responsible are the award-winning Newlands Cross Cemetery Buildings; Newlands Cross Crematorium; the rebuilding of Cong Church; the oratory at the Blanchardstown Centre; Knock House Hotel; the refurbishment of Knock parish church; the CAT-scan unit in Letterkenny General Hospital, and private housing, including the House in Adare Manor. He was involved in the preparation of the development control plan for Letterkenny General Hospital and has participated in competitions, including those for the new Tallaght Hospital and the new basilica at San Giovanni Rotondo in Italy. He is currently involved with the Glasnevin National Heritage Project and with the design of tourism housing in Powerscourt. He has been a member of the Royal Institute of Irish Architects since 1980 and was elected a Fellow in 2006. He was accredited a Conservation Architect in 2003.

KEITH MEGHEN

Keith Meghen graduated as an architectural technician from Dublin Institute of Technology in 1993 and completed a diploma in project management in 2002. He has been with A&D Wejchert & Partners since 1995, and was made an associate in 2001. Previously, he worked with Lisney Building Surveyors. He is responsible primarily for healthcare projects, including various projects in Our Lady of Lourdes Hospital, Drogheda, Naas General Hospital, Connolly Hospital and Brookfield Health Centre. He has also worked on residential and commercial projects, such as House in Adare Manor, Limerick; Chief O'Neill's Hotel, Smithfield; O'Rahilly Building, University College Cork,; a mixed development at Tone Street, Ballina, and the Blanchardstown Shopping Centre. He is also responsible for in-house computer and networking management of the practice. He is a technician member of the RIAI since 1999.

WADE SUTTON

Wade Sutton graduated in South Africa with a National Technician Diploma in architecture in 1990. He joined A&D Wejchert & Partners at the end of 2000 and was made an associate in 2007. Over the past 16 years he has specialised in healthcare environments and has worked for leading healthcare organisations worldwide. He has worked on projects such as Our Lady of Lourdes Hospital, including the symptomatic breast unit/palliative care, out-patients department, midwifery-led unit, oncology department upgrade, ICU and CCU, as well as Sligo Acute Mental Health Care Unit, Naas General Hospital, Tullamore General Hospital and the acute psychiatric unit at Ennis Hospital.

CURRENT AND FORMER STAFF (as in January 2008)

A&D Wejchert & Partners gratefully acknowledge the valuable contribution of current and former staff members who have helped the practice become what it is today. It is hoped that all are included in the listing which follows.

CURRENT STAFF

Darragh Breathnach
Deborah Burke
Peter Carroll
Brian Cashin
Alister Corbett
Stephen Crowley
Mariana Deus
Matthias Deutsch
Pritesh Durgapersad
Brian Glaholm
Paul Glinka
Fergal Kelly
Anthony King
Marion Kraus
Ewa Kulik
Jacek Lojek
Pawel Luczejko
Siobhán McEvitt
Marian Minarik
Eddie Mullally
Emer O'Leary
Brendan O'Donovan
Monika Porebska
Carl Stanford
Tomasz Stasiak
Mas Zakaria

FORMER STAFF

Dermot Bannon
Brendan Barry
Paul Barry
Ian Black
Linda Brady
Tomasz Brzecki
Merrit Bucholz
Thomas Byrne
Ross Cahill-O'Brien
Ben Campbell
Robert Carroll
Enda Cavanagh
Gordon Chisholm
Turlough Clancy
Brian Cleary
Denis Connolly
Orla Connolly
Catriona Coyle
Tom Creed
Cathy Dalton
Cahir Davitt
Kate Dempsey
Paul Derham
John Bosco Dillon
Colm Dunphy
Seán Feeney
John FitzGerald
Herbert Gebhardt

Sorcha Geoghegan
Tom Gilsenan
Martin Gittens
Noel Gorman
Derek Grey
Padraic Halligan
Derek Hennessy
Patrick Hennessy
Ali Jay
Jong Joo Tze
Perry Kelly
Lewis Kwok
Paul Lally
Jim Luke
Denis Lutzow
Barry Lyons
Art McCormack
Suzanne MacDonald
Peter McDonnell
Kieron McGrath
George McMullen
Leeanne Marshall
Fionnuala May
Stephen Moore
Joe Mulvey
Michael Murphy
David Murphy
Mary Murray
Sandra Nolan
Paul O'Callaghan
Fionnuala O'Connor
Peter O'Donnell
Darina O'Farrell
Derek O'Leary
Garrett O'Neill
Peter O'Donoghue
Michael O'Farrell
Sarah O'Keeffe
John O'Reilly
Marie O'Sullivan
Pat O'Sullivan
John Pearson
Mattias Peretz
Stephen Perkins
Emmet Power
Eamonn Ryan
Gerry Salley
Kai Sander
Gabriel Silke
Tracey Sludds
John Somers
Michael Somers
Noel Tobin
Michael Walsh
Agnieszka Wejchert-Pearson
Mateusz Wejchert
Grace Weldon
Craig White

Awards & Distinctions

ARCHITECTURAL COMPETITIONS

1964	International Competition for the New Campus for University College Dublin, and for Arts, Administration and Aula Maxima buildings	1st Prize
1974	Department of Education Community School Architectural Competition	2nd Prize
1975	Dublin Diocesan Church Competition	highly commended
1982	Abbey Homesteads House Design	commended
1988	International Competition for Basilica for 10,000 pilgrims, San Giovanne, Italy	4th place
1989	Ericsson Competition, Athlone	3rd Prize
1996	International competition for Aquarium in Nouméa, Nouvelle Calédonie	shortlisted
1997	Stillorgan Shopping Centre, Dublin – limited competition	1st Prize
1997	Redevelopment of Ilac Centre, Dublin 1 – limited competition	1st Prize

OTHER AWARDS AND DISTINCTIONS

1973	RIAI Triennial Gold Medal, 1971-73	Administration Building, UCD
1976	International Timber Architectural Award – 3rd prize	Community pre-school
1979	Shannonside Environmental Award for best commercial building built in last 5 years	Aillwee Cave Visitor Centre
1980	Plan Building of the Year Award	Aillwee Cave Visitor Centre
1980	Europa Nostra Diploma (presented by President of Ireland, Dr Hillery at Áras an Uachtarain on 21 January 1982, for an 'outstanding contribution to the conservation and enhancement of Europe's architectural and natural heritage')	Aillwee Cave Visitor Centre
1981	An Taisce commendation	Aillwee Cave Visitor Centre
1982	Mont Kavanagh Award for Investment Architecture – commendation	Small Industrial Units, Clonshaugh
1983	Sunday Independent Arts Award for outstanding achievement in industrial architecture	AnCo Training Centre
1984	An Taisce Context Awards – public building category – industrial building category – ecclesiastical category – commendation	Sports Building, UCD AnCo Training Centre Parish Church, Blessington
1984	Plan Building of the Year Award	AnCo Training Centre
1985	National Rehabilitation Board Building Design Awards 1983-84 (new buildings category) – commendation	AnCo Training Centre
1986	RIAI Triennial Gold Medal 1977-79 – commendation	Aillwee Cave Visitor Centre
1987	Plan Building of the Year – Regional Award	Office Building. IDA, Castletroy
1989	RIAI Triennial Gold Medal, 1980-82 – highly commended	Sports Centre, UCD
1990	RIAI Regional Award	Psychiatric Unit, Naas General Hospital
1992	RIAI Regional Award Plan Building of the Year Award National Drywall Award BREEAM Environmental Friendly Award	Office Development, 65-66 Lr Mount Street Beresford Court (Irish Life) Beresford Court (Irish Life) Beresford Court (Irish Life)
1996	European Building Construction Excellence Award Plan Building of the Year – Regional Award	Student Centre, UCC Student Centre, UCC
1998	ICAD Annual Awards Environmental & Production, Design, Interior – bronze	Old Jameson Distillery Museum

1999	Opus Building of the Year Award – commended	Chief O'Neill Hotel
	Glen Dimplex Design Award – nomination	Chief O'Neill Hotel
	'Life in Architecture' Competition	
	– best public building in Warsaw in 1998-99	Sobanski Palace Complex
2000	Minister of Culture of Poland – diploma for	
	best modernisation of a historical complex	Sobanski Palace Complex
2000	Opus Building of the Year Award	
	– highly commended	Newlands Cross Cemetery Buildings
2000	RIAI Regional Award	Newlands Cross Cemetery Buildings
2000	Opus Building of the Year Award – commended	Luke Wadding Library, WIT
	Minister for Environment's Sustainability Award	Luke Wadding Library, WIT
2002	Polish Ministry of Infrastructure	
	– Building of the Year – 2nd prize	Media Business Centre (ITI)
2002	Opus Building of the Year Award	
	– commended,	Quinn Direct
2003	Intelligent Buildings Award	Media Business Centre (ITI)
2003	British Council of Shopping Centres	
	– Established Centre Award	Blanchardstown Centre
2003	Irish Concrete Society Award – building category	The Helix, DCU
	Irish Joinery Awards – 1st prize (for joinery at O'Mahony Hall)	The Helix, DCU
	Opus Building of the Year Award	The Helix, DCU
2004	Opus Building of the Year Award – special mention	House at Ardcarraig
2004	Irish Concrete Society Awards – elemental category	Irish Cement Offices
2005	Opus Building of the Year Award – commended	Walton IT Building, WIT
2006	Opus Building of the Year Award	
	– highly commended	Nurse Education Building, WIT
2007	Dept of Environment, Heritage & Local	
	Government Best Sustainable Project	Nurse Education Building, WIT
2007	RIAI Irish Architecture Award	Nurse Education Building, WIT

Exhibitions

LIST OF PROJECTS EXHIBITED AT PUBLIC EXHIBITIONS

YEAR	EXHIBITION	PROJECT
1980	*Sense of Ireland*, London	Holy Trinity Church
		Aillwee Cave Visitor Centre
		Ballincollig Community School
		Administration Building, UCD
1981	UIA (International Union of Architects)	
	XIV Congress Exhibition, Warszawa	Aillwee Cave Visitor Centre
1981	Urban Renaissance, Cork (RIAI exhibition)	Mathematical / Science, UCC
1984	*An Taisce Context Awards*,	Sports Building, UCD
	National Concert Hall, Dublin	Parish Church, Blessington
		AnCo Training Centre
1986	*New Irish Architecture*, Taylor Galleries, Dublin	Sports and Leisure
		Centre, Greystones
1986	*Architecture in Ireland*, Helsinki	AnCo Training Centre
		Aillwee Cave Visitor Centre
		Sports Building, UCD
1986	*Maisons Individuelles*, Athens	House at Loughrask, Co Clare
	(CLAEU exhibition)	
1987	UIA XVI Congress Exhibition, Brighton	Aillwee Cave Visitor Centre
		Sports Building, UCD
		AnCo Training Centre
1989	*The Architect and the Drawing –*	AnCo Training Centre
	150 years of RIAI members' work 1839-1989,	Aillwee Cave Visitor Centre
	(touring exhibition)	The Peak, Hong Kong

1990	RIAI Regional Awards Exhibition	Naas General Hospital Development Plan
1992	RIAI Regional Awards Exhibition	Beresford Court (Irish Life) Office Development, 65-66 Lr Mount St
1994	Royal Hibernian Academy 164th Annual Exhibition RHA Gallagher Gallery, Dublin	20th-Century Museum
1996	*Building on the Edge of Europe*, Maison de l'Architecture, Paris	Beresford Court (Irish Life) Office Development, 65-66 Lr Mount St Aillwee Cave Visitor Centre 20th-Century Museum
1996	RIAI Regional Awards Exhibition	Student Centre, UCC
1997	*20th-Century Architecture: Ireland*, German Architecture Museum, Frankfurt	Aillwee Cave Visitor Centre
1997	RIAI Regional Awards Exhibition	Blanchardstown Centre
1998	RIAI Regional Awards Exhibition	Swords Health Centre Aeronautical and Environmental Technology Building, UL Old Jameson Distillery Museum
1999	RIAI Regional Awards Exhibition	Retail Park, Blanchardstown Addition to Residence at Monkstown
2000	RIAI Regional Awards Exhibition	Sobanski Palace Complex
2001	RIAI Regional Awards Exhibition	Luke Wadding Library, WIT Newlands Cross Cemetery Buildings Smithfield Village
2000	*Panoramas Européens 2000*, Paris (Arsenal Pavilion)	Smithfield Village
2002	UIA XXI Congress Exhibition, Berlin	Sobanski Palace Complex
2003	RIAI Regional Awards Exhibition	The Helix, DCU
2004	*About the House*, RTÉ	House at Ardcarraig
2004	RIAI Architecture Awards Exhibition	Medical Business Centre
2005	*About the House*, RTÉ, 2005	Heather Cottage, Howth

2005	RIAI Architecture Awards Exhibition	Walton IT Building, WIT House at Ardcarraig
2006	*Wspolczesna architektura Warszawy* (*Contemporary Architecture in Warsaw*), Warsaw, Vienna, Budapest, Berlin	Sobanski Palace Complex
2007	RIAI Architecture Awards Exhibition	Nurse Education Building, WIT

Bibliography

LIST OF PROJECTS PUBLISHED IN PROFESSIONAL
JOURNALS AND BOOKS

JOURNAL	PROJECT
Architects' Journal, The (UK)	
—— 157/15, 11 Apr 1973	University College Dublin
—— 167/12, 22 Mar 1978	Ballincollig Community School
—— 169/12, 21 Mar 1979	Holy Trinity Church
—— 170/34, 22 Aug 1979	Aillwee Cave Visitor Centre
—— 174/47, 25 Nov 1981	Sports Centre, UCD
Architectural Record (USA)	
—— Aug 2002	Sobanski Palace Complex
Architectural Review (UK)	
—— CLIX, 947, Jan 1976	Ballincollig Community School
—— CLXIII, 971, Jan 1978	Preview '78: Holy Trinity Church
—— CLIXVIII, 1001, July 1980	Holy Trinity Church
Architecture (USA), AIA Journal 3rd Annual Review	
of World Architecture, Sep 1984	AnCo Training Centre
Architecture in Ireland	
—— Jun 1978	Administration Building, UCD
Architecture Ireland	
—— 160, Sep 2000	Newlands Cross Cemetery Buildings
—— 166, Apr 2001	Luke Wadding Library, WIT
—— 181, Oct 2002	Quinn Direct
—— 183, Jan 2003	The Helix, DCU
—— 183, Jan 2003	R Ryan, 'A&D Wejchert
	in Ireland and Poland'
—— 196, Apr 2004	Media Business Centre
—— 202, Nov 2004	Irish Cement Offices
—— 212, Nov 2005	Walton IT Building, WIT

—— 213, Jan 2006	D Kornaus-Wejchert,
	'Designing for Health'
—— 224, Feb 2007	Nurse Education Building, WIT
see also *Irish Architect*	
Architecture To-day (UK)	
—— 167, Apr 2006	Arigna Energy Centre
Architekt (Poland)	
—— Apr 2000,	interview with A&D Wejchert
—— Jan 2002	Newlands Cross Cemetery Buildings
	Waterford Institute of Technology
—— Aug 2004	South King Street Development
	Connolly Hospital
Architektura (Poland)	
—— Apr 1973	University College Dublin
—— Dec 1986	Interview with A & D Wejchert
—— Feb 2000	Sobanski Palace Complex
—— Mar 2000	Sobanski Palace Complex
—— Apr 2003	The Helix, DCU
—— Sep 2003	Media Business Centre
—— Oct 2003	The Helix, DCU
l'Architettura (Italy)	
—— 227, 17 Sep 1974	Universita degli Studi della Calabria
Build (UK)	
—— Nov 1972	University College Dublin
Building (UK),	
—— 6766, 2 Feb 1973	University College Dublin
Building Design (UK)	
—— 26 Aug 1977	Ballincollig Community School
—— 11 Jan 1980	Water Tower, UCD
Building for Learning (AAI, Dublin, 1986)	
	International Business Centre, Castletroy
	Plassey Technological Park
	South County Business Park
Building Specification	
—— Nov 1975	Ballincollig Community School
Building with Steel (UK)	

—— Dec 1979	Holy Trinity Church
The Bulletin, ACUI (USA)	
—— Mar 1997	Student Centre, UCC
Business and Finance	
—— Nov 1991	Beresford Court (Irish Life)
Concrete Quarterly (UK),	
—— 123, Oct-Dec 1979	Aillwee Cave Visitor Centre
—— 124, Jan-Mar 1980	Water Tower, UCD
—— 127, Oct-Dec 1980	Holy Trinity Church
Construction	
—— 9/13, Feb 1980	Water Tower, UCD
—— Dec 1991	Office Development, 65-66 Lr Mount St
Construction Trade	
—— Mar 1998	A & D Wejchert Architects
Education Times, The	
—— 3/44, 30 Oct 1975	Ballincollig Community School
European Building	
—— July-Aug 1993	interview with A& D Wejchert
	Singapore Science Park
—— Jun 1996	Student Centre, UCC
Farbe und Raum (Germany)	
—— 2 Feb 1980	Ballincollig Community School
FX International Interiors (UK)	
—— Oct 1999	Galway County Council Hall
	Chief O'Neill Hotel
Habitation Space (Switzerland)	
—— 2, 1980	International Hotel in Abu Dhabi
House	
—— Spring/Summer, 2005	Heather Cottage, Howth
Industry, Magazine for Irish Industry	
—— Sep 1984	Office Building, South County Business Park
L'Industria Italiana del Cemento	

— 10, Oct 1982   Sports Centre, UCD

Irish Architect
— 64, Nov 87-Jan 88   Custom House Docks
— 71, Mar-Apr 1989   San Giovanni Rotondo, Italy
— 77, Mar-Apr 1990   Ericsson Competition
— 79, Jul-Aug 1990 Psychiatric Unit, Naas General Hospital
— 87, Nov-Dec 1991   Office Development, Lr Mount St
— 88, Jan-Feb 1992   Beresford Court (Irish Life)
— 90, May-Jun 1992   Robert Schuman Building, UL
— 98, Nov-Dec 1993   Knock Apparition Chapel
— Dec 1995   Blanchardstown Centre
— May 1996   Student Centre, UCC
— Feb 1997   Blanchardstown Centre
— Nov-Dec 1997   Swords Health Centre
— April 1998   Old Jameson Distillery Museum
— May 1998   Aeronautical & Environmental Technology Building, UL
— Oct 1998   Addition to Residence at Monkstown
— Jan 2000   Sobanski Palace Complex
— Jan 1999   Oratory in Blanchardstown Centre
— Jun 1999   Galway County Council Hall
— May 1999   Chief O'Neill Hotel
see also *Architecture Ireland*

Irish Arts Review
— Nov 2002   The Helix, DCU
— Autumn 2003   Galway County Council Hall
— Autumn 2005   Heather Cottage, Howth

Irish Bystander
— Mar-Apr 1981   Sports Centre, UCD
— Apr-May 1981   University College Dublin
— Jan 1982   Holy Trinity Church, Dublin
    Parish Church, Blessington

Irish Construction Industry Magazine
— Sep 1992   Beresford Court (Irish Life)

Journal of the American Concrete Institution
— Jul-Aug 1980   Water Tower, UCD

Journal of the National Association of College Auxiliary Services (USA)
— Jun 1997   Student Centre, UCC

Landscape Architecture, American Society of Landscape Architects
— 74/4, Jul-Aug 1984   Landscape of campus at UCD

Materia Revista d'Architectura (Italy)
— 28, 1998   Blanchardstown Centre

Mayazyn Budowlany (Poland)
— 6, 2000   Sobanski Palace Complex

Nikkei Architecture (Japan)
— 9/3, 1979   interview with A&D Wejchert

New Civil Engineer (London)
— 337, 1980   Water Tower, UCD

Office Age, Integrated Magazine for the Office and Urban Environment (Tokyo)
— 20 1993   Beresford Court (Irish Life)

Plan (Dublin)
— 2/4, Jan 1971,   University College Dublin
— 6/4, June 1975   Interview with A&D Wejchert
— 6/8, Nov 1975   Ballincollig Community School
— 8/1, Sept 1976   Dublin Diocesan Church Competition
— 8/10, Aug 1977   Ballincollig Community School
— 9/1, Jan 1978   Administration Building, UCD
— 10/1, Jan 1979   Holy Trinity Church
— 10/11 & 12, Dec 1979   International Hotel, Abu Dhabi
    Small Industrial Units, Clonshaugh
    Aillwee Cave Visitor Centre
— Aug 1980   Aillwee Cave Visitor Centre
— 12/9, Sep 1981   Sports Centre, UCD
— 12/3, Mar 1981   Lombard & Ulster Bank
— 12/7 & 8, Jul-Aug 1981   AnCo Training Centre
— 13/2, Feb 1982   Aillwee Cave Visitor Centre
— 14/11, Nov 1983   AnCo Training Centre
— Plan Building of the Year 1983   AnCo Training Centre
    House at Loughrask
— 15/10, Oct 1984   Dalkey School Project
    South County Business Park
    Office Building, Leopardstown
    Castletroy International Business Centre
    Office Building, Castletroy

    Parish Church, Blessington
    House for Jane Norris, Loughrask, Co Clare
    The Peak, Hong Kong – Competition
    Howth Yacht Club – Competition
— 17/3, Mar 1986   Second Level School, Brookfield
— 5/90, May 1990   Psychiatric Unit, Naas General Hospital
— 1/92, Jan 1992   Fitzwilliam Lawn Tennis Club
    Beresford Court (Irish Life
— 10/96, Oct 1996   Student Centre, UCC
— Jun 2006   Ballymun Health Centre

Plastica (Italy)
— 32/2, Feb 1979   Ballincollig Community School

Progressive Architecture (USA)
— Jan 1965   University College Dublin

Project Management
— Aug2001   Newlands Cross Cemetery Buildings

Projekt (Poland)
— 3, 1980   National Library, Teheran
    Water Tower, UCD
    House for Herbert von Karajan
    International Organisations Centre
    International Hotel in Abu Dhabi
    Design for Playschool in Timber
    Arts / Commerce Building, UCD
    Ballincollig Community School
    Holy Trinity Church
    Administration Building, UCD

RIBA Journal (UK)
— Oct 1981   House at Kilbogget, Killiney

Share
— 25, 1999   Oratory in Blanchardstown Centre

Stratum, NDP magazine
— Dec 2002   Review of recent work by ADW – Connolly Hospital
    Luke Wadding Library, WIT

Sunday Times – Culture section (Dublin)

—— 18 Nov 2001   Newlands Cross Cemetery Buildings

Ulster Architect (Belfast)
—— 10/3, Jan-Feb 1989   interview with A&D Wejchert

Voice of Padre Pio (Italy)
—— XIX, 4, 1989   San Giovanni Rotondo, Italy

World Water (USA)
—— Jan 1980   Water Tower, UCD

——

BOOKS   PROJECT

l'Architecture Formes Functions (Anthony Kraft, Switzerland)
—— 16 (1971)   interview with A&D Wejchert
                 International Organisations Centre
                 University College Dublin

Build Your Own House
(Dyflin Publications, Dublin, 2005)   House at Ardcarraig

Contemporary Architecture (Anthony Kraft, Switzerland)
—— 4 (1982-83)   Sports Centre, UCD
—— 6 (1984-85)   AnCo Training Centre

Contemporary Irish Church Architecture
by Richard Hurley, Wilfred Cantwell (Gill & Macmillan, Dublin, 1985)
                 Holy Trinity Church

Dublin: A Guide to Recent Architecture
(RIAI, Dublin, 1996)   Office Development, 65-66 Lr Mount St
                 Holy Trinity Church
                 Beresford Court (Irish Life)

The Encyclopedia of Ireland
(Gill & Macmillan, Dublin, 2003)   biography of A Wejchert

Environmental Design: the best of architecture and technology
by Margaret Cottom-Winslow (New York, 1990)
                 Aillwee Cave Visitor Centre
                 Ballincollig Community School
                 Holy Trinity Church

Office Building, South County Business Park
                 The Peak, Hong Kong

Façades de Maisons Individuelles
by Jean-Pierre Dumont (Editions Delta & Spes, Belgium, 1985)
                 House at Loughrask

Irish Architectural Review, 3
(RIAI/Gandon, 2001)   Newlands Cross Cemetery Buildings
                 Smithfield Village
                 Luke Wadding Library, WIT

Irish Hospital Architecture
(Dept of Health & Children, 1997)   Swords Health Centre

The New Housing
(RIAI, Dublin, 2002)   Smithfield Village

150 Years of Architecture in Ireland: RIAI 1839-1989
(RIAI, Dublin, 1989)   Water Tower, UCD
                 Sports Centre, UCD
                 Holy Trinity Church
                 Ballincollig Community School

Rooftop Architecture
(NAI Publishers, Rotterdam, 2005)   Smithfield Village

20th Century Architecture: Ireland
(Prestel, Munich / New York, 1997)   Aillwee Cave Visitor Centre

Who's Who in Ireland
ed. Maureen Cairnduff (Kevin Kelly, Dublin, 1991, 1999)   biography

Who's Who in the World
(Macmillan Directory Division, USA, 1992)   biography

DID: International Directory of Architecture & Design (UK, etc)
—— 3 (1994)   Beresford Court (Irish Life)
                 Robert Schuman Building, UL
                 Office Development, 65-66 Lr Mount St
                 Student Centre, UCC
—— 4 (1996)   Student Centre, UCC
                 Knock Apparition Chapel
                 Blanchardstown Centre
—— 5 (2000)   Blanchardstown Centre
                 Media Business Centre (ITI)
                 Swords Health Centre
                 Old Jameson Distillery Museum
—— 6 (2003)   The Helix, DCU
                 Luke Wadding Library, WIT
                 Galway County Council Hall

——

note: books and periodicals published in Ireland unless otherwise stated

Photography

A&D Wejchert & Partners gratefully acknowledges the contribution of the following photographers in the documentation of its work over the decades:

Arcaid
Fabienne de Backer
Hélène Binet
Michael Blake
Donach Photography
Patrick Donald
Derek Fannin
Bill Hastings / Arc
Irish Times
Kingram Studios
Wojciech Krynski

Barry Mason
Peter Moloney
David Murphy
Ronnie Norton Associates
Finbarr O'Connell
Gerry O'Leary
Louis Pieterse / PDI
Henk Snoek
C Tkaczyk
Vincent Vidal
Neil Warner

Index

BUILDINGS + PROJECTS